THE CROSSROADS COUNTRY

BY

THOMAS ALEXANDER

The Crossroads Country by Thomas Alexander

Direct Light Publishing
45 Dudley Court, Endell Street, London, WC2H 9RF

Permissions may be sought directly from Publishing Rights Department 45 Dudley Court, Endell Street, London, WC2H 9RF
performance@directlight-publications.com

Library of Congress Cataloguing in Publication Data
Application submitted.
British Library Cataloguing in Publication Data
Application submitted.
04 05 06 07 08 10 9 8 7 6 5 4 3 2
ISBN 978-1-941979-10-5

The characters and events in this book are fictitious. Any similarity to real persons, living or dead, is coincidental and unintended by the author.

Edited by Shirin Laghai for Direct Light Publications.

Cover design by SimplyA

DIRECT

LIGHT

THE CROSSROADS COUNTRY

Synopsis

Blending quotes and actual events with fictional dialogue, The Crossroads Country dramatizes the last thirty years of Afghan history up to and including the attacks of September 11, 2001, and the subsequent invasion.

Merging international intrigue with the life of a single Afghan family the play utilizes humour and music as a backdrop to the international catalysts that conceived, created, and implemented the birth of global terror.

Why did the Soviets invade Afghanistan? Why did the Americans fund the Jihad? Why did Osama bin Laden go to Afghanistan? Who funded the Taliban? And why was Massoud killed two days before 9/11?

With over a hundred historical characters and well over a thousand quotes The Crossroads Country is a fast paced political play that provides an open door to anyone interested in current events as a detailed overview of Afghan history to students of this era and an innovative, informative, and entertaining theatrical experience.

ABOUT THE AUTHOR

Thomas Alexander has worked in almost all forms of theatre, from opera to children's performances, working as everything from stage hand to costume designer, and has seen his work translated into four different languages and performed as far afield as America and Afghanistan.

His plays, along with his first novel, *A Scattering Of Orphans*, have been published by Direct Light Publications.

Also by the Author

PLAYS

Happiness
Murder Me Gently
The Family
Begat
The Crossroads Country
Great
The Visitor
When Dusk Brings Glory
The Recruitment Officer
Writer's Block
The Last Christmas
Writing William
The Big Match

ONE ACT PLAYS

Four Widows and A Funeral
For Arts Sake
The TV
Life TM
The Dance

ADAPTATIONS

William Shakespeare's' R3
Othello

NOVELS

A Scattering Of Orphans

FOREWORD

When I first pitched the structure of The Crossroads Country to the then Aghan Ambassador to Japan Haron Amin, I took with me three plays: Stuff Happens, by David Hare, Frost/Nixon, by Peter Morgan, and Copenhagen, by Michael Frayne. I also had a copy of Julius Caesar in my bag but was worried that might be taken the wrong way, so I don't believe I passed it on.

My point was this: a play, on a fixed stage, with little-to-no budget can tell both an intimate and a global story, tell it well, and educate while entertaining. You don't need to talk down to people. You don't need to cut things out. You can provide a theatrical experience that no one will forget and hope, if nothing else, to start a dialogue.

You didn't, as I was quick to point out to the Ambassador, simply have to do The Kite Runner all over again.

The Crossroads Country comes from a million sources, some first-hand, others from books too numerous to name here. It would be folly to claim the research as my own in any true sense. After all, it is not the role of a dramatist to act as journalist, but rather to elucidate, through the text, the myriad of work done by the million journalists and researchers gone before.

The question must then be asked: to what degree must the dramatist be true to the facts? To what degree can he be allowed to sacrifice reality for the sake of the narrative?

What, when all is said and done, is 'true' about a play?

The Crossroads Country is, to the best of my knowledge, true to the facts. I'm not sure which came in ahead in the final tally: my words or quotations, but I know that it was a close run thing, and I also know that the funnier the line, the more preposterous, the more liable it is to be a direct quotation.

Nevertheless, I wasn't there. I wasn't in the Politburo in 1979 or in the White House in 1999. I wasn't in Bagram in 2005 and I certainly wasn't in New York in 2001. So the question must be asked: what do I know?

Fiction trumps reality. We see this every day, and this is never more true than when it comes to dramatizations. Richard III may have had a limp, Brutus may have been an honourable man, C.S. Lewis may have had a wardrobe in his attic, and Mark Zuckerberg may have screwed over his only real friend due to a lack of self-worth, but all have been disputed. There is a movie at the present moment doing the rounds about Jimi Hendrix in which he is portrayed as an abusive partner, despite the fact that the woman in question disputes the events completely. A film based on the life of Stephen Hawking has been challenged for portraying his wife as if the writer had made her up, despite being based on a biography, written by her.

It is, in the words of Aaron Sorkin, the duty of the artist to captivate you for however long we've asked for your attention. If we stumble into truth, we got lucky. And we don't get to decide what truth is. However, both Mozart and Salieri would probably disagree.

History isn't written by the victor. It's written by the dramatists employed by them. At the end of the day the poets, singers, painters, and writers have the last say, and what they say will far outlast any kind of journalistic integrity that is strived for. Queen Elizabeth II's life will be remembered through Peter Morgan. The death of JFK will be remembered through Oliver Stone. Margret Thatcher through Abi Morgan, and probably even Nelson Mandela through William Nicholson, amongst others.

Stories are in our nature. They are how our brain works. We look for patterns in chaos and build narratives from them. An artist will often claim that the 'truth' is the 'truth' of the experience, not the events, but when it comes to world events, where people lived and people died, where reputations are built and legacies are destroyed, perhaps we should be looking for a little more.

An artist – and I do not claim myself among them – is a window to the world. And though we may be stained, it is our duty to at least try to let some light in.

Thomas Alexander – 2014

The following is the cast list as played at the June 16 premier in Tokyo, 2009. Parts, however, can be altered as fit.

Justin Berti	Zahir Shah, Father, Massoud, Man, Teacher
Patrick Smith	Ambassador, Andropov, Daoud, Crewman, Ayoub, Shevardnadze, Richardson, Guard
Antun Percec`	Carter, Casey, Old Man, Clinton, Akhromeyev, Ghafoozi
Mish'al Samman	Amin, Turki, Saaya, Zia, Khalili,
Anastasia Van Allen	Mother, Militant 2, Admin, Albright, Hazara 4, Audience 1
Ian Platt	Brezhnev, Gorbachov, Simons, Ubadiah, Rabbani, Simons, Wasel, Hazara 3
Bob Werely	KGB, Ustinov, Corporal, Omar, Ambullah, Hazara 2
David Mashiko	Haq, Taraki, Vaughn Forrest, Fadl,
Ron Scott	Director, Brezinski, Advocardos, Pilot, Inderfurth, Audience 3
Lazlo Kotazek	Gromyko, Commander, Hafs, Akhtar, Kryuschev, Hazara 1, Iman,
Jon Reimer	Vance, Dubs, Bearden, Wilson, Clarridge, UN Worker, Qualdrani
Nico Minas	Soldier 2, Statesman 2, Deligate 2, Fred Ikle, Taliban 1, Quanzi, Audience 2
Cyrus Sethna	Solder 1, Statesman 1, Deligate 1, Gromyko, Masob, Barbar, General, Taliban 2, Rama, Touzani, Audience 3
Kimberly Tierney	Aide, Snowflake, Nurse, Militant 1
Chris Parham	Howard Hart, Marty Millar,
Aditi Nayar	Deligate 3, Bhutto,
Arlene Dinglasan	Audience 4, Leila
Thomas Ireton	Teen, Tameem
Andres Clark	Boy
Michael Mitchell	AJT
Soprano	Akiko Otao

STAGE ABREVIATIONS

CONT.	The same actor continues speaking
V/O	Voice Over (recorded voice)
OFF	Actor is off stage
TA	Actor speaks directly to the audience.
SOTTO	Sotto Voce
BEAT	Slight pause indicating thought.

THANKS

Many, many thanks must go out to Haron Amin, whose dedication and drive inspired both the inception of the play and many of the ideas contained within.

Further thanks must go to the staff at the Afghan Embassy in Tokyo, including the incomparable Jason Pratt for their help and acccess during the research period of the play. I treasured my time with them and think of them often.

The original presentation of the play would not have been possible without the inspirational people at Tokyo International Players, including, but not limited to, the wonderful Andrew Woolner, Graig Russell, and Jonah Hagans, who deserve all good things.

Finally, I have to thank the incredibly talented Mish'al Samman and his company, Miraj Productions, who helped walk me through the minefield of Middle Eastern diplomacy and rhetoric, as well as creating the original production material for the play.

THE CROSSROADS COUNTRY

ACT ONE

ACT ONE

SCENE 1

CHAIR AND DESK CENTRE STAGE. TYPEWRITER IN THE CENTRE.

ENTER TOYNBEE (AJT)

HE TAKES HIS PLACE AT THE TABLE, LOADS A PIECE OF PAPER INTO THE TYPEWRITER, AND BEGINS TO TYPE.

AJT   From a European standpoint, all roads lead to Rome. But Europe is one of the fringes of the Old World, and eccentric positions produce distorted views. The roads leading to the civilization of the old world, sheered to Sleppa and Begran, or Syria and Afghanistan respectively. Seen from this central position, the road-map of the Old World will assume a very different pattern.

HE SITS BACK, THINKING, AND LIGHTS A CIGARETTE.

AJT   It is obvious that Afghanistan is intensely interesting today for a student of contemporary international affairs. It is of equal interest for a student of the history of civilization in the Old World during these last five thousand years. As he follows the main threads of history – economic, political, demographic, artistic, religious – he finds his attention being drawn again and again to the Old World's eastern crossroads, as well as its western one. The examples of Afghanistan's role as a crossroads in each of these aspects are so numerous that an exhaustive catalogue would fill a volume and would quite overload a chapter. A few illustrations will be enough to make the point.

AS HE WRITES A SCREEN DROPS DOWNSTAGE, COVERING HIM.

A MOVIE, PROJECTED DOWN ONTO THE SCREEN STARTS. A COUNTDOWN, IN OLD MOVIE STYLE, IS STARTED: 5, 4, 3, 2…

SCREEN: A MAP OF EURASIA, AFGHANISTAN CENTRE.

AJT   By the end of the nineteenth century, Afghanistan has once again become the centre of the political world. 'The Great Game', played out around its borders between the great bear of Russia and the Lion of England, have caused turmoil and bloodshed throughout the region.

THE SCREEN SHOWS THE LION OF ENGLAND, TRAILING RED ACROSS THE MAP, MOVING OVER WHAT IS PRESENTLY INDIA AND PAKISTAN, MOVING UP INTO AFGHANISTAN UP UNTIL THE DURAND LINE, WHILE THE BEAR OF THE PRUSSIAN EMPIRE PAINTS BROWN INTO MODERN DAY RUSSIA.

AJT   In 1933 however...

SCREEN: THE   COLOURS   OF   THE   FLAG   OF AFGHANISTAN   FLOOD   INTO   THE   COUNTRY, OVERTAKING THE ENGLISH RED, AND SPREAD OUT, FILLING ITS BORDERS.

AJT (CONT.)   Despite strained relations between England and Afghanistan over the creation of the state of Pakistan, a new time of peace and prosperity starts, led by King Zahir Shah.

LIGHTS   COME   UP   BEHIND   THE   SCREEN,   BACK-LIGHTING AN ACTOR AS HE STANDS RAISED AND CENTRE, CASTING HIS SHADOW OUT THROUGH THE CLOTH OF THE SCREEN.

ZAHIR SHAH   It will be the longest period of peace our country has ever seen. The best rulers, I am told, are always benign dictators. The problem is whoever comes next.

AJT   In 1973 however, the king is deposed by his brother-in-law; Mohammed Daoud Khan who becomes the country's first president.

THE ACTOR PLAYING THE KING IS TOPPLED, AND REPLACED BY ANOTHER.

DAOUD   Five years! He gets forty years and all I get are five lousy years? Personally I blame the Russians.

AJT   The president's fear of the support garnered by the People's Democratic Republic of Afghanistan, a Soviet backed political party, leads to arrests, assassinations, and in April 1978, an uprising. President Daoud is killed, along with his family.

BEHIND THE SCREEN MEMBERS OF THE PDPA ARE CHASED AND SHOT BY GOVERNMENT TROOPS. MORE PEOPLE TAKE THE STAGE, WAVING FLAGS AND SHOUTING SLOGANS FOR THE PDPA.

PRESIDENT DAOUD IS TOPPLED FROM HIS POSITION AND, WHILE LIT BY A SINGLE SPOTLIGHT, SHOT.

BACK-LIGHTS DOWN.

SCREEN: A MOVIE OF KABUL, CIRCA APPROXIMATELY LATE NINETEEN SEVENTIES, IS SHOWN, THE CITY RESPLENDENT.

AJT   What started as a decade of hope and prosperity for Afghanistan has come to an end. The role of America in Iran and the suspicions of the cold war have moved the country from a beacon of hope and prosperity for the Islamic world, into what will become the battlefront for civilization.

SCENE 2

THE SCREEN RISES. A SMALL SPOTLIGHT ON A MAN – THE FATHER - CENTRE STAGE, DIGGING IN HIS GARDEN, EXPANDS TO FILL THE STAGE.

FROM OFF WE HEAR A TANNOY, ANNOUNCING THE OVERTHROW OF PRESIDENT DAOUD AND THE INSTIGATION OF THE PDPA.

FATHER PAUSES AND THEN CONTINUES DIGGING.

HIS BOY RUSHES IN, CARRYING THE NEW FLAG (PDPA) OF AFGHANISTAN.

ENTER BOY.

BOY   Baba jan, look!

ENTER MOTHER.

MOTHER   Stay out of the dirt!

FATHER   What have you got there?

BOY   It's our new flag!

FATHER   What is it?

BOY   Our new flag. The People's… (HE CAN'T
REMEMBER) The People's….

FATHER   Go fetch me an apple.

MOTHER   Go on!

EXIT BOY.

MOTHER   There are tanks.

FATHER   In the street?

MOTHER   They've taken over the government. Here.

                SHE HANDS HIM A PAMPHLET.

FATHER   The People's Democratic Party of Afghanistan.

MOTHER   Do you know them?

FATHER SHAKES HIS HEAD, AND CONTINUES READING.

FATHER   Taraki? This is Khalq. They've taken over the
government?

MOTHER   They are saying Daoud is dead. You can hear them
even here. Who are they?

FATHER   Communists. I… This is not good. Daoud… These
people could not form an agreement, let alone a government. If
they're… The only way they could have done this is with Soviet
backing.

MOTHER   We should leave Kabul? Go to the village, just
until this settles.

FATHER   It will be no safer. No, if they have the government…
There is nothing we can do, and Daoud was far from perfect. We will
just have to wait and see what communism means in the context of
Kabul.

ENTER BOY.

BOY   (HOLDING OUT AN APPLE) Baba jan.

FATHER   (TO MOTHER) We will be fine.

EXIT MOTHER.

FATHER (CONT., TO BOY) Come here.

HE TAKES THE APPLE AND A KNIFE FROM HIS POCKET AND STARTS TO CUT OFF THE FLESH, PASSING IT TO HIS BOY AS HE DOES SO.

BOY   What are we doing?

FATHER   We are planting.

BOY   An apple tree?

FATHER   Just so. Most people, when they are looking to plant a tree, they cut away everything from the apple, digging out the pips with a blade of a knife. This is not right. The flesh is not just there for us. It is for the pips as well. It is what nourishes them, nurtures them, you understand? What you have to do is make a window, just a window, help the pips. Give them an escape, you understand? But leave the core. You must always leave the core, otherwise the tree will not grow. Then, when you have your window, you bury it, like so. (THE TWO BURY THE APPLE CORE. THE TANNOY STOPS) You put it in firm ground, not soft, but you must not pack it too hard. It must feel, for the apple, as though it fell from the tree, rolled down the hill and came to rest. If it knows it is buried, it cannot grow. (FINISHED) And then you leave it.

BOY   And it will grow.

FATHER   If the conditions are right. If it wants to bad enough. You must be patient.

BOY   For how long?

FATHER   For a tree?

BOY   How long?

FATHER   (STANDING) Until you are this tall.

ENTER MOTHER.

MOTHER ENTERS STAGE RIGHT.

MOTHER   Wash your hands.

FATHER   Come.

THEY ALL EXIT STAGE RIGHT AS THE SOVIET FLAG

DESCENDS.

SCENE 3

INSIDE THE KREMLIN.

ENTER BREZHNEV AND AN AIDE.

BREZHNEV STRIDES DOWNSTAGE PURPOSELY, PASSING PAPERS BACK TO HIS AIDE IN DISDAIN.

BREZHNEV   (SHOUTING) No! No. I want actual figures, you understand me! Actual figures!

AIDE   Comrade Secretary, these are actual…

BREZHNEV   Accurate figures. Not (HE THRUSTS THE PAPERS INTO THE HAND OF THE AIDE) these!

AIDE   Comrade Secretary, these are the figures…

BREZHNEV   The KGB does not run Afghan policy. Where is Andropov? Hmm? Why isn't Andropov here? The Politburo runs Afghan policy, the Kremlin runs Afghan policy!

AIDE   Comrade Andropov is aware of the facts…

BREZHNEV   Facts? Yes. He is aware of the facts. I am not aware of the facts. That is what I am saying. The people are not in receipt of the facts!

ENTER ANDROPOV.

ANDROPOV   Comrade Secretary General.

BREZHNEV   There you are. What are these?

ANDROPOV   I do not…

BREZHNEV   Do not play coy with me, Comrade Andropov. I am still Secretary General.

ANDROPOV   I cannot see what you are holding from this distance, Comrade Secretary.

BREZHNEV   (MOVING TOWARDS HIM) I asked for actual

figures. On Afghanistan.

ANDROPOV   You have to understand, Comrade Secretary; things change daily and our intelligence in the region isn't exactly…

BREZHNEV   (CUTTING HIM OFF) Go on. Finish that sentence. (GRABBING A PIECE OF PAPER) I have here a request from this Tareki.

AIDE   Taraki, Secretary General.

BREZHNEV   Asking for (READING) sixteen tank divisions. Sixteen tank divisions! And this is the twelfth such request since they took office!

ANDROPOV   May I? (HE READS) Well, obviously this is out of the question.

BREZHNEV   Is it? Is it!? They seem to be under the impression that we are helping them, are they not?

ANDROPOV   We've helped them so far, we pull out now it will just destabilize the region. Is it not the purpose of the Soviet nation to aid in the great experiment wherever it takes place?

BREZHNEV   (SNORTINGLY) Great experiment. What did I say? What did I say? "The transformation of a traditional society can only be achieved extremely slowly, and certainly not by wrecking its existing structure and relationships." If there is one country in the world where we would not like to try scientific socialism, it is Afghanistan!

ANDROPOV   You also said, Secretary General, that when external and internal forces hostile to socialism try to tear down the regime, it is a common problem for all socialist states. The Soviet Union cannot allow this revolution to fail.

BREZHNEV   Harrumph. How many backers do this PDPA have in the military?

ANDROPOV   In Afghanistan? When they took power, probably no more than about a thousand.

BREZHNEV   And now?

ANDROPOV   Probably twice that number. Another 15,000 civilian supporters.

BREZHNEV   A handful!

AIDE   No wonder they are asking for tanks.

BREZHNEV   Which we cannot send! America…

ANDROPOV   Agreed.

BREZHNEV   What is this infighting I hear about?

ANDROPOV   There are factions. Before the takeover. Two groups. Parcham and Khalq. Khalq have the power…

BREZHNEV   This is Tareki?

ANDROPOV   Taraki, yes. Many Parcham supports have already been rounded up and killed. The first…

BREZHNEV   Law of any revolution, is to kill all counter revolutionaries. Yes I know. Lenin's ghost, they take their handbooks seriously.

ANDROPOV   Indeed. There are uprisings. In the remote regions at the moment but they will spread. There is no doubt about that.

BREZHNEV   We cannot send Soviet tanks.

ANDROPOV   Agreed.

BREZHNEV   How many, actual figures, how many does the KGB have placed in the military?

ANDROPOV   Personnel or paid?

BREZHNEV   Round it up for me.

ANDROPOV   Throughout the whole country, no more than five thousand.

BREZHNEV   Harrumph. (BEAT) This infighting cannot continue. They need to understand that.

ANDROPOV   Yes, Secretary General.

BREZHNEV   Make them understand. They do not have the number to do what they want to do.

ANDROPOV   I shall.

BREZHNEV   And make sure these insane proposals remain that as well, comrade: proposals. Proposals are all well and good, but these start getting put into practice and there's going to be all out civil war.

ANDROPOV   As you say, Comrade Secretary.

BREZHNEV   What is he calling himself, this Tareki?

AIDE   Taraki, Comrade Secretary.

SCENE 4

THE WHITE HOUSE.

VANCE   The Great Teacher! Shit, these boys really know how to go all out with their titles don't they? The Great Teacher, the Great Leader. Great, great, great. What do they think they are, Britain?

AIDE   It sounds better in Russian.

ENTER BRZEZINSKI.

VANCE   It would damn well have to, wouldn't it? You see this Zeb?

BRZEZINSKI (TA) By the end of 1978 the infighting amongst the communist party has led to thousands of arrests and assassinations, with several influential and prominent leaders seeking asylum in the Soviet Union for fear of the death squads that President Taraki has organized throughout the capital.

For the Carter administration, spearheaded by Secretary of State John Vance and special advisor Zbignew Brzezinski, the news is not wholly without its silver lining.

BRZEZINSKI   Has the president seen this?

VANCE   Not yet.

BRZEZINSKI   And these figures are (BEAT) accurate?

VANCE   According to the ISI.

BRZEZINSKI   Eighteen thousand. What do they think they are, Stalin?

VANCE   I was more interested in the reforms.

BRZEZINSKI   We've heard this before.

VANCE   This time they're pushing it through.

BRZEZINSKI   (INTERESTED) Really?

VANCE   Land reforms, Marxist behaviour, everything.

BRZEZINSKI   Well, that is good news.

AIDE   (SINCERE) I agree.

VANCE   The Soviet's aren't going to let Afghanistan fall. Not after all this.

BRZEZINSKI   Which is exactly the point. You start destroying the landlord class and Moscow will have no recourse but to invade.

AIDE   I'm sorry, Mr. Secretary. We… We are talking about the same thing. Land's… I thought America was for women's rights and private ownership?

THE OTHER TWO LAUGH.

VANCE   You'll have to forgive my young friend here. Harvard isn't what it used to be.

BRZEZINSKI   The PDPA are communist. You do know what communists are, right? They are funded… Hell, they're controlled by the KGB.

AIDE   All the same…

VANCE   It's the first steps of a Marxist revolution.

BRZEZINSKI   (TICKING OF POINTS) Create a working class, end the feudal system, centralize the government.

VANCE   The great experiment. (BEAT) And there it is again. Great.

AIDE   I still don't see…

BRZEZINSKI   Zahir talked about it for years. And it's all very well when that's all it is; talk. Keep Moscow happy, appease the secularists.

VANCE   Except the country isn't secular. Isn't ready for it.

BRZEZINSKI   Know much about Islam, son?

11

AIDE   I… I have a masters in political geography. From Berkeley.

BRZEZINSKI   I'll take that as a no. You can't just walk into a country and change one thousand years of system overnight. It would take… thirty years…

VANCE   Thirty years at least.

BRZEZINSKI   …America or the Soviets, to turn a feudal system into… whichever one you want.

VANCE   Thirty years at least.

BRZEZINSKI   This is going to piss Brezhnev off no end. Eighteen thousand? These arrest figures are correct?

VANCE   Near as we can tell.

BRZEZINSKI   This is great news.

VANCE (TA)   Brzezinski said in his book, 'The Geostrategic Triad', published in 2000…

BRZEZINSKI   (ADDRESSING THE AUDIENCE) The full story of the productive US-China cooperation directed against the Soviet Union, especially in regard to Afghanistan, initiated by the Carter Administration, still remains to be told.

VANCE   Did you speak to the Shah?

BRZEZINSKI   Pahlavi? This morning.

VANCE   What did you tell him?

BRZEZINSKI   What do you think I told him? I told him we'd back him to the hilt.

VANCE   Are you sure that's wise?

BRZEZINSKI   Not if I meant it. No. Let's take this to the President.

SCENE 5

AFGHANISTAN.

A SCHOOL HOUSE. SCHOOL DESKS LINE THE SIDES OF THE THEATRE. BOYS TAKE THEIR PLACES IN THEM, LOUD AND RUDE.

ON THE TABLE ARE PAPER MACHE MOUNDS.

UPSTAGE IS A PICTURE OF PRESIDENT TARAKI.

A TEACHER ENTERS UPSTAGE CARRYING A KALASHNIKOV WHICH HE PLACES ON THE TABLE.

TEACHER (SHOUTING) Art!

THE ROOM QUIETS.

TEACHER (CONT.) Art is central to Afghan culture. Can anyone tell me why? No, I didn't think so. (HE BEGINS TO STRIDE DOWN STAGE) Along with reading and maps and arithmetic you will all learn to express yourselves through art. This is not decadence. This is not 'an easy class'. Afghanistan is home to Mahmud of Ghazni and his 400 poets and 900 scholars. It is the home to Sanaee, Rumi, and Ansar. It is even the home to Ahmed Zahir. (THERE ARE LAUGHS FROM THE CHILDREN) For a man to be a man he must… he must what? Tameem?

TAMEEM   He must be a poet and a warrior.

BEHIND THE TEACHER'S BACK THE BOY THROWS SOME PAPER MACHE AT TAMEEM. THE CLASS STIFLES A GIGGLE. A FURTIVE PAPER MACHE FIGHT STARTS BEHIND THE BACK OF THE TEACHER.

TEACHER   This is a time of change. Great change. The Great Teacher himself has ordered that education is for everyone. Not just for ignorant boys. Education, and art, is to be one of the cornerstones of the new Afghanistan…

THE BOY, THROWING PAPER AT ONE OF THE OTHER BOYS, MISSES AND HITS THE PICTURE OF TARAKI.

THE TEACHER TURNS.

TEACHER (CONT.)   And Sculpture is one of the cornerstones of art. Today… (HE NOTICES THE PICTURE, STOPS) What is this? What is this? Which of you shayetan threw this? Speak! This is the Great Teacher! This is... Who threw this? I demand to know now. (SILENCE) I demand... If I do not... The Great Teacher is bringing change to Afghanistan. He is bringing the future to Kabul and you shadi think it is fun to deface him like that. Do you? Do you? I will know who did this! I will know who thinks he is greater than our President. And I will know; now! Was it you? Hmm? You? Hold up your hands. HOLD UP YOUR HANDS! If you have paste... (ALL BOYS HAVE PASTE ON THEIR HANDS. THE BOY STARTS TO LAUGH) You think this is funny? You're laughing?

BOY   No, Agha.

TEACHER   You think defacing the leader of your country, a good man, is funny!

BOY   No, Agha.

TEACHER   Did you do this? (SILENCE) Tell me. Did you do this. I will not be angry. I just want to know, it's alright. Did you do this?

TAMEEM   (STANDING) I did it.

THE TEACHER TURNS AND LOOKS AT HIM. HE'S NOT THE BOY HE WANTS.

TEACHER   You.

TAMEEM   I am sorry Malem Saheb.

THIS, HOWEVER, INFURIATES THE TEACHER. HE STRIDES ACROSS TO THE BOY.

TEACHER   Come here.

GRABBING TAMEEM BY THE EAR THE TEACHER MOVES DOWN THE DESKS DRAGGING THE SCREAMING CHILD WITH HIM. HE THROWS HIM AGAINST THE SIDE OF THE TEACHER'S DESK AND, ROUNDING IT, PICKS UP A RULER.

TEACHER   Put your hand on the table. (TAMEEM DOESN'T RESPOND) Put your hand on the table! (TIMIDLY HE DOES SO. THE TEACHER POINTS AT THE PICTURE) This man is a great man. This man will bring freedom, he will bring reform and he will bring education to the people of Afghanistan.

TAMEEM   Yes, Malem Saheb.

BOY   Malem Saheb.

TEACHER   Does he deserve to be treated like this?

BOY   Malem Saheb!

TEACHER   Does he deserve your disrespect?

TAMEEM   No, Malem Saheb.

BOY   Malem Saheb.

TEACHER   Does he?

THE TEACHER BRINGS THE RULER DOWN ON THE BOY'S HAND. THE BOY SCREAMS, AND BLOOD SPLATTERS ONTO THE TABLE.

TAMEEM PULLS BACK HIS HAND IN PAIN.

TEACHER   Put your hand back there! (NO RESPONSE) Put your hand back there!

BOY   Malem Saheb!

THE TEACHER TURNS TO THE BOY, SILENCING HIM WITH A STARE, THEN RETURNS TO TAMEEM

TEACHER   Change must come with pain. This we learn, yes? Respect must be won, if it cannot be found. It must be won by the mighty, and it must be won with blood. Do you understand? (TAMEEM NODS) Then put your hand back there.

TAMEEM MOVES HIS HAND BACK OVER THE TABLE AND THE TEACHER MOVES TO STRIKE AGAIN.

BLACKOUT.

SCENE 6

AFGHANISTAN.

ANDROPOV (TA)   In February 1979, the Islamic Revolution in Iran destabilized what was already a unstable game of chess between the USA and the USSR. The overthrow of the American backed Shah Mohammed Pahlavi and the rise of the Ayatollah put the already fragile PDPA in a delicate position. Islamic protesters had already launched a number of raids along Afghanistan's border states and to the Taraki-led government, already divided in its approach to Marxist reform, being surrounded by Islamic militants must have seemed a lot less inviting than the seemingly stable balance of Russia on one side and America on the other.

BRZEZINSKI (TA)   An international incident seemed inevitable. And it came in the form of the kidnapping of Adolph Dubs, the American Ambassador by four militants in a Kabul Hotel.

ENTER DUBS AND FOUR COMMUNIST MILITANTS.

DUBS IS DRAGGED ONTO THE STAGE TO A CHAIR PLACED CENTRE. DUBS IS FORCED TO SIT, AND IS HANDCUFFED TO THE CHAIR.

ONE OF THE MILITANTS BEGINS TO READ.

DUBS   The American people…

A MILITANT HITS HIM, HARD.

MILITANT ONE   Shut up.

MILITANT TWO   America's interference in the region cannot and will not be tolerated by the people of Afghanistan. The Marxist revolution will not be stopped. The people will not allow the Great Satan to dictate policy to the people of Afghanistan. The great experiment and the freedom of people from the tyranny of religion and greed demands that we take this action.

DUBS (TA)   The incident creates problems for both the KGB and the White House.

LIGHTS UP ON TWO TABLES, ONE IN THE WHITE HOUSE, ONE IN THE KREMLIN. ANDROPOV AND BRZEZINSKI ARE BOTH TALKING ANIMATEDLY INTO PHONES.

ANDROPOV   Where are they?

BRZEZINSKI   Mr. President. President Carter is asking, and frankly, he's expecting restraint on this issue.

ANDROPOV   How many agents are there?

BRZEZINSKI   I cannot impress upon you any stronger…

ANDROPOV   Is the hotel secure?

BRZEZINSKI   …how important it is that this not become any bigger a crisis than it already is.

ANDROPOV   The Americans cannot be seen to have any influence on this matter. The CIA…

BRZEZINSKI   The American people have lost too much already.

ANDROPOV   Our reports are the CIA already have a team working in Iran. If they were to…

BRZEZINSKI   I can promise you, Mr. President; human rights are of the highest importance to President Carter…

ANDROPOV   Well what kind of influence do you have over them?

BRZEZINSKI   If the government were to open a dialogue with these terrorists…

ANDROPOV   The Afghan government cannot be seen to talk to these comrades. Any appeasement of the left will only…

BRZEZINSKI   I understand that the Afghan government cannot be seen to negotiate with terrorists, but…

ANDROPOV   The important thing is to put an end to it, and put an end to it now.

BRZEZINSKI   (SHOUTING) …but you do it all the time!

ANDROPOV   Storm the building.

ANDROPOV HANGS UP.

BRZEZINSKI   Mr. President, restraint in this matter…

COMPLETE BLACKOUT.

THERE IS SHOUTING FROM THE MILITANTS. THE SOUND OF GUNFIRE IS HEARD AND MUZZLE FLASHES SHOW BOTH THE MILITANTS AND DUBS DYING IN A HAIL OF BULLETS.

ONE OF THE MILITANTS, WOUNDED, SCREAMS IN PAIN.

A FLASHLIGHT LIGHTS THE FALLEN MAN WHO IS SHOT.

LIGHTS UP.

THREE OF THE MILITANTS AND DUBS ARE DEAD. A FOURTH HAS ESCAPED.

SOLDIERS ARE SEARCHING THE ROOM.

SOLDIER 1   Where is the fourth man? There were four of them! Where is the fourth man!

SOLDIER 2   Comrade Commander; it appears he has escaped down the fire escape.

SOLDIER 1 (TA) In order to cover up the escape, an innocent prisoner is executed in his place and blamed for the death of Dubs, live on TV.

A PRISONER IS DRAGGED ONTO THE STAGE AND MADE TO KNEEL CENTRE STAGE.

PRISONER   I stole a car stereo.

THE PRISONER IS SHOT AND HIS BODY DRAGGED OFF.

THE SCREEN DESCENDS AT THE FRONT OF THE STAGE.

SCENES FROM THE IRANIAN HOSTAGE CRISIS ARE PLAYED OUT ON THE SCREEN.

SOLDIER 2   American outrage is so strong that international aid to the country is all but cut off, leaving the more remote parts of the country even more stranded and at odds with the Taraki government.

The incident also shapes the Carter administration's approach to the Iranian hostage crisis.

SCENE 7

THE SOVIET UNION.

SOLDIER 1   Along the border with Iran, news of the Ayatollah's return bolsters anti-Russian sentiment. In the moderate Islamic town of Herat, for centuries an enclave of spiritualism and learning, an entire regiment rebels.

BREZHNEV IS SEATED AT HIS DESK SIGNING ORDERS.

BREZHNEV (TA)   In response to the mounting problems in Afghanistan, the Kremlin calls President Taraki to Moscow for talks with Secretary Brezhnev. The talks are aimed at stabilizing the country and preventing further Soviet involvement.

ENTER ANDROPOV AND USTINOV.

ANDROPOV   He's here.

BREZHNEV   Let him wait. (PAUSE) What's he like?

USTINOV   Charming. Too charming.

BREZHNEV   Yes, I thought he might be. Well, where are we on this anyway?

ANDROPOV   Bearing in mind that we will be labelled as an aggressor, but in spite of that, under no circumstances can we lose Afghanistan.

BREZHNEV   It won't come to that.

USTINOV   It's already coming to that. The problem is that the leadership of Afghanistan does not sufficiently appreciate the role of Islam. It is completely clear to us that the country is not ready at this time to resolve all of the issues it faces through socialism. The economy is backwards, the Islamic religion predominates, and nearly all of the rural population is illiterate.

BREZHNEV   Yes, but what is to be done!

ANDROPOV   The only thing that can be done at this time is to try to unite the party. Stop these inward squabbles. If the arrests keep up the only socialists left in the country will be the ones we put there.

USTINOV   And they're getting killed by the Islamics.

BREZHNEV   Yes, yes. Alright. Show him in. Who's the other one?

ANDROPOV   Amin.

BREZHNEV   And we're sure Taraki is our man.

ANDROPOV   (SHRUGGING) He, at least, is charming.

BREZHNEV   Alright. Show him in.

USTINOV GOES TO THE DOOR AND RE-ENTERS WITH TARAKI. BREZHNEV GREETS HIM WARMLY.

ENTER TARAKI.

BREZHNEV   Comrade Taraki. How do you like our Moscow autumns?

TARAKI   I think you would prefer our Kabul springs Comrade Secretary.

THEY SHAKE HANDS.

BREZHNEV   Please, sit. (JOKING) You would like something for the heat, perhaps?

TARAKI   Some water?

BREZHNEV NODS TO USTINOV AND HE POURS WATER.

BREZHNEV   How was Cuba?

TARAKI   What they are doing there… It is exhilarating. Exhilarating!

BREZHNEV   You should have been there twenty years ago. You met with Castro?

TARAKI   Quite a man.

BREZHNEV   An old warrior. But then, we are all old warriors, are we not. You've met Comrade Andropov of the KGB?

TARAKI   Of course.

BREZHNEV   And Comrade Ustinov? (TARAKI NODS) Well, let's get down to it shall we? Comrade Taraki. This situation in Afghanistan…

THERE IS SILENCE.

TARAKI   Comrade Secretary. I will not lie to you. The situation is getting worse. Whole areas of Herat are almost wholly under the influence of Shiite slogans. Since the Iranian revolution…

ANDROPOV   Do you have the forces to oust them?

TARAKI   I wish that were the case. If, Comrade Secretary, if I had the military assistance…

USTINOV   Hundreds of Afghan officers were trained in the Soviet Union. Where are they all now?

TARAKI   Most of them are Muslim reactionaries. We have

no confidence in them.

BREZHNEV   This is not what we want to hear.

TARAKI   I have a solution.

BREZHNEV   Go on.

TARAKI   We… the Afghan government, need troops.

ANDROPOV   We cannot give you troops. Such an incursion…

TARAKI   But you can! In disguise. Why can't the Soviet Union send Uzbeks, Tajiks, and Turkmens in civilian clothing? No one will recognize them! They could drive tanks because we have all these nationalities in Afghanistan. Let them don Afghan dress and wear Afghan badges and no one will recognize them. Iran and Pakistan are already doing the same thing for the guerrillas.

USTINOV   You are, of course, oversimplifying the issue.

ANDROPOV   Afghanistan's Islamic rebellion is a far more complex and political issue.

BREZHNEV   The USSR cannot send troops across a border into a sovereign nation. Not without conquering it. However… We can supply you with additional, how shall we call them? Advisors. Training. Along with MILITANT 1-24 helicopter gunships. Weapons. Guns… But these battles; Jalaalabad, Faizabad, Bamian. They must end. And end swiftly. A socialist movement, once started, cannot be stopped. Do you understand?

TARAKI   We will deal with them most harshly.

BREZHNEV   Yes, I'm sure you will. Then there's the question of…

ANDROPOV   The government. These attacks… You are at war with your own country! These attacks will continue until you have a democratic coalition government.

BREZHNEV   Listen to me. Comrade. We know the teachings of Lenin. But Afghanistan… This is not the right time. You are moving too fast. You must unite the party. Free political prisoners, make contact with Barak Karmel, and….

USTINOV   Remove Amin.

BREZHNEV   Prime Minister Amin.

USTINOV   Deputy Prime Minister...

ANDROPOV   The Khalq regime is in danger of imminent collapse.

BREZHNEV   We have... How did you call it?

ANDROPOV   Scripts.

BREZHNEV   Indeed, scripts, for this. Ways of going about it that won't raise attention from inside the party. (HE RISES) Come, go with me. If I sit too long my feel get cold. We will walk and we will tell you what to say.

USTINOV   The Great Teacher can become the Great Student.

ANDROPOV GLARES AT HIM.

BREZHNEV   You drink vodka, Comrade?

EXIT BREZHNEV, ANDROPOV, AND USTINOV

SCENE 8

THE WHITE HOUSE.

ENTER PRESIDENT CARTER AND BRZEZINSKI.

CARTER (TA)   Meanwhile, in the White house the opinion of the failing government is...

CARTER IS READING SOMETHING, BRZEZINSKI FOLLOWING. THEY HEAD TO THE SAME DESK THAT BREZHNEV WAS AT BEFORE.

BRZEZINSKI   This is their Vietnam, Mr. President.

CARTER   And the mullahs...

BRZEZINSKI   Mujahideen, Mr. President.

CARTER   These guys are on our side?

BRZEZINSKI   Well, no, Mr. President. They're not on anyone's side. Except their own and God's.

CARTER   The Islamic God.

BRZEZINSKI   Allah. Yes, Mr. President.

CARTER   How can I be funding Islamists after Iran?

BRZEZINSKI   This is… That's oversimplifying it, Mr. President.

ENTER VANCE.

CARTER   (TO VANCE) What do you think Vance?

VANCE   Mr. President?

CARTER   Zeb wants us to start funding the Mujahideen.

BRZEZINSKI   Mr. President. The CIA…

VANCE   This is Afghanistan?

CARTER   Zeb here thinks it's going to be their Vietnam.

VANCE   I thought Vietnam was their Vietnam.

BRZEZINSKI   From the other side.

CARTER   See, I just don't know. I mean, we're supposed… What happened to humanitarianism. Aren't we supposed to be pushing humanitarianism?

BRZEZINSKI   There's always a humanitarian at one end of a bullet, Mr. President.

CARTER   And SALT? What if this gets back to us?

BRZEZINSKI   It won't. Mr. President. You have the recommendation from the CIA. The whole thing will be run out of Pakistan, and the king will match every cent we put in, dollar for dollar.

CARTER   This is Saudi Arabia?

BRZEZINSKI   Mr. President. Think about it. This is a country that's already this close to overthrowing its government. A Soviet backed government. They're about as communist as you or I! They're this close to throwing out the PDPA and all they need is a little monetary push. But if the Soviets send in more helicopters…

VANCE   Jesus, Zeb. You're talking about an arms build-up! Right when we're in the middle of SALT, you're talking about an arms build-up!

BRZEZINSKI   I'm talking about the biggest hit the Soviets have ever taken. If Afghanistan falls... Mr. President. We lost Iran. Let's make them lose Afghanistan.

VANCE   And what if it doesn't? What if they invade?

BRZEZINSKI   Then they get their own private Vietnam. An Islamic country under the thrall of a Soviet government? They'll be fighting there for years!

VANCE   And we'll be funding them!

CARTER   I'm gonna do it.

VANCE   Mr. President!

CARTER   (SIGNING THE PAPER) No, I'm gonna do it. Zeb's right. It's not like we want the place, but the Soviets. They can't let this go.

VANCE   They'll invade.

CARTER   Maybe they will, maybe they won't, but we get Iran, they're going to get Afghanistan. And God help them. Whichever God they can find.

BRZEZINSKI (TA)   On July 3rd 1979, President Carter signs a secret initiative to help fund the Mujahideen. A full five months before the Soviet Invasion of Afghanistan.

SCENE 9

AFGHANISTAN.

TARAKI (TA)   Upon return to Kabul, Taraki calls Deputy Prime Minister Amin to his office for what is ostensibly an ice-breaking meeting. Amin, in the company of the Soviet Ambassador who is invited in order to promote unity, arrive at the palace early. Reports of what happened at the meeting are disparate.

AMIN   (ADDRESSING THE AUDIENCE) I am not a violent man. But I am an educated one.

TARAKI   The idea was to poison him.

AMIN   History has taught us that enemies come with handshakes.

TARAKI   Once he was inside the palace we were going to fake a coup and shoot him.

AMIN   Frankly, though, I have been plotting this for years. I have a great many fellows inside the Great Teacher's staff and a trip to Moscow does not go unnoticed, if you know what I mean.

TARAKI   We were hoping for peace! One last chance at a sit down. I was only going to exile him if he didn't.

AMIN   I brought the Russian Ambassador. It seemed like a good move at the time. If anyone could protect me from his 'teaching' it was the Russians.

AMBASSADOR I had no idea what was going on. The KGB run Afghanistan. No one told me anything about a gun fight.

TWO ARMED GUARDS APPEAR BEHIND TARAKI.

TARAKI   Mr . Deputy Prime Minister.

AMIN   (DRAWING A GUN) Mr. President.

AMIN SHOOTS AT TARAKI, THE GUARDS RETURN FIRE. BOTH MEN WITHDRAW TO THE WINGS. THE AMBASSADOR REMAINS CROUCHED CENTRE STAGE, BEWILDERED AND AFRAID.

AMBASSADOR (TA) The meeting is adjourned and Amin escapes. Within days, however, he returns with a garrison of soldiers and storms the building.

SOLDIERS FROM EITHER SIDE FIRE ON EACH OTHER, AMIN IN THE CENTRE OF HIS FORCES, TARAKI BEHIND HIS.

TARAKI'S GUARDS FALL OR SURRENDER EASILY, AND TARAKI IS DRAGGED INTO THE MIDDLE OF THE STAGE.

AMBASSADOR (TA)   It is months before the death of the Great Teacher is announced to the public. Ill health is the official reason for his withdrawal from public office; though in all probability, this is simply a formality.

TARAKI   And it was such a good script too…

TARAKI IS SHOT AND FALLS DOWN, DEAD.

AMBASSADOR (TA)   When the Soviet world awakes the next morning, it finds a new dynamic in place in Afghanistan, the head of which the KGB and Kremlin alike were plotting to have removed.

For the people of Kabul, it is a sign of the ever-growing fragility of the PDPA. Two violent coups within eighteen months, one of which within its own party, is seen as a signal of decay.

Protests are met with harshly, in the capital and beyond. Purges of Taraki's followers and the release of previously jailed Amin supporters lead to violent clashes and assassinations. For all but the blinkered, a crisis can only be a matter of time.

Battles with the Mujahideen and Islamic forces along the borders, and the ever growing reach of the Soviet Union, lead to a rash of refugees crossing the border. Civil war has started in all but name, and in the capital many prepare for the inevitable showdown.

SCENE 10

AFGHANISTAN.

LIGHTS UP ON THE MOTHER, CENTRE STAGE. THE FATHER RETURNS HOME FROM WORK.

FATHER   Where is he?

MOTHER   He's upstairs.

FATHER   What did they say?

MOTHER   They didn't say anything, aziz, and it's not just them. There… Some of the shops are closed down.

FATHER   Did you see the pigeons?

MOTHER   Pigeons?

FATHER   They're all over the city. They painted them red. Thousands of them. Everything's red.

MOTHER   The store was full, it was just closed.

FATHER   And they didn't say anything?

MOTHER   Nothing.

FATHER   At the school, I mean. They didn't say anything?

MOTHER   He's been crying since he got home.

FATHER   It's the two E's, expulsion or execution. Even the city is…

MOTHER   We should leave. Others are talking about it.

FATHER   This is our home.

MOTHER   We could go to America. They…

FATHER   He's upstairs?

MOTHER   (BEAT) Yes.

FATHER   Send him down here.

EXIT MOTHER.

FATHER STAND CENTRE STAGE, TENSE. THE BOY RUNS ON AND CLINGS TO HIS FATHER WHO BENDS DOWN TO TALK TO HIM.

ENTER BOY.

FATHER (CONT.) Hey now. What is this? Look at me. Look at me! This is not what men do. This is not how a man behaves. (THE BOY WIPES HIS EYES) That's better.

ENTER MOTHER.

MOTHER WATCHES CAREFULLY.

BOY   They wouldn't say what happened. I went to his house but it's empty. All the things are there but there's no lights.

FATHER   This is Tameem?

THE BOY NODS.

BOY   Tameem, Abdul, and Sebqhatullah. The teacher cleared their desks. He said this is what happens to boys who don't learn.

MOTHER   He's not going back…

SHE SEES HER HUSBAND AND STOPS.

FATHER   Have you seen the pigeons? (THE BOY SHAKES HIS HEAD) You haven't seen the red pigeons? Pigeons are red now, did you know that? No more grey pigeons. No more white pigeons. Only red. Can you believe that? (THE BOY SHAKES HIS HEAD) Get your coat. Cats, I think, will be green. Would you like to see a green cat? A pink horse? No? Grab your coat and we'll go and take a look. (TO MOTHER) We'll go for a walk. See the red pigeons.

EXIT BOY.

MOTHER   I hate red.

FATHER   (NODDING) The rain will wash it off.

MOTHER   And if it doesn't?

FATHER   It can't last.

MOTHER   That's what I'm afraid of.

SCENE 11

MOSCOW.

ENTER ANDROPOV AND USTINOV.

ANDROPOV   She tells me he is barely aware of the world around him.

USTINOV   The nurse?

ANDROPOV   All he talks about are his medals. Medals. As if they mean anything.

USTINOV   And she is KGB.

ANDROPOV   Of course she is KGB. Do you think I would entrust the care of the Secretary General to anyone else but the KGB. She is KGB.

USTINOV   Which drug is it anyway?

ANDROPOV   What do I look like? A chemist? Nembutal.

USTINOV   That's a sleeping pill.

ANDROPOV   (IMPRESSED BUT WARY) Indeed.

USTINOV   You think…

ANDROPOV   Not before the Olympics. And not before SALT II either. It would look like a coup.

USTINOV   Americans. The arrogance of them. A build-down in nuclear weapons while they fund guns to their satellites.

ANDROPOV   The world needs to see the Soviet Union in a new light, Dmitriy. It is… The world is changing. This is what they tell me. It is changing. (BEAT) Let it. We will do what we can with the left hand, while doing what we need to with the right, yes?

USTINOV   This transparent funding of the Mujahideen alone…

ANDROPOV   The Mujahideen are not our problem.

USTINOV   If they continue to fi…

ANDROPOV   The Mujahideen are not our problem! Our problem is that we cannot be drawn into a war with Afghanistan. Not now! The Czechs…

USTINOV   The Czechs are our problem.

ANDROPOV   This Amin is our problem! I send officers to his office, he does not see them, and when he does see them, he talks nothing, nothing of consequence!

USTINOV   This is what will happen when a man knows you have tried to kill him.

ANDROPOV   That was months ago! Anyway, he cannot be so blind as to think he does not need the KGB. (PAUSE) You know he has withdrawn himself from Kabul?

USTINOV   I didn't. No.

ANDROPOV   He has withdrawn himself almost completely. Family, friends… It's an impossible situation.

USTINOV   Perhaps he should be removed.

ANDROPOV   (THINKS) We tried that.

USTINOV   Poison?

ANDROPOV   He has his own family members tasting his food for him. What kind of man has his own family members tasting his food for him?

USTINOV   A prudent one.

ANDROPOV   A twelve year old boy we nearly killed. I ask you.

USTINOV   Something less subtle then?

ANDROPOV   We already shot at him.

USTINOV   Yes. I read that. Who did we use?

ANDROPOV   A Turkmen.

USTINOV   Turkmens can't shoot.

ANDROPOV   This, I know.

USTINOV   A Russian would have…

ANDROPOV   Yes, yes. What we need is something more… subtle.

USTINOV   It can't look like the Soviet…

ANDROPOV   It has to be within his own party. The PDPA have to remove him themselves. This close to the Olympics…

USTINOV   Not to mention SALT II.

ANDROPOV   The Soviet Union cannot be seen to have a hand in…

PAUSE.

USTINOV   Amin studied in America.

ANDROPOV   He did, didn't he.

USTINOV   There are still many within the PDPA who might be able to infer something from that.

ANDROPOV   (NODDING) CIA.

USTINOV   It would explain the coup. Limit him from his base.

ANDROPOV Is he that unpopular?

USTINOV The opposite. But still…

ANDROPOV He is a CIA plant. The Great Satan. This will… The Islamics, the PDPA!

USTINOV He will be completely alone.

ANDROPOV Who is our man here. The Afghani?

USTINOV Karmal.

ANDROPOV He is good?

USTINOV He is a good communist.

ANDROPOV Do we control him?

USTINOV Is winter freezing in the Urals?

ANDROPOV We need him in control. Before the end of the year.

USTINOV Amin is CIA. America is looking to take over Afghanistan now it has lost Iran.

ANDROPOV Before the end of the year! We have enough problems as it is.

USTINOV You are going to SALT?

ANDROPOV I want to meet this Brzezinski. I hear he is something of a chess player.

USTINOV Wrap up warm, Comrade. Summers in Washington are like winters in the Ural.

LIGHTS DOWN ON MOSCOW.

LIGHTS UP ON THE WHITE HOUSE.

BRZEZINSKI IS TALKING ON THE PHONE.

BRZEZINSKI A – M – I – N, I'm holding it in my hand! He's the President of Afghanistan for crying out loud. (BEAT) Well, get a map. I want all your head of station… I want the Director to send me all details of contact between the CIA and President Amin, and I want it now! Before and after he 'took' office. (PAUSE) Yes, all of them, what are you deaf? He studied here in the US I want all records of any approaches made to him in college, all records of any dealings with him while he was Deputy Prime Minister, and all dealings we've had with him after the coup. (PAUSE) Because I'm holding in my hand a communiqué from our office in Kabul telling me he's a CIA operative, that's why! And for reasons passing understanding he's asked to meet with two representatives from our embassy. (PAUSE)

Yes I have a clearance code. (BEAT) Well, it'd be a little too clear if I told you what it is over the phone now, wouldn't it? You do remember Watergate?

ENTER TWO STATESMEN AND AMIN.

TWO STATESMEN ENTER STAGE RIGHT, PASSING IN FRONT OF BRZEZINSKI. FROM THE LEFT AMIN COMES IN, MEETING THEM CENTRE STAGE. THE THREE SHAKE HANDS AND SIT.

BRZEZINSKI   B-R-Z-E-Z-I-N-S-K-I. (BEAT) Zbignew. (SIGH) Z-B-I….

LIGHTS DOWN ON THE WHITE HOUSE.

AMIN   Sit, sit.

THE THREE SIT.

AMIN (CONT.) Tea?

AMIN (TA)   The meeting with the American representatives remains one of the worst political blunders made by the sitting president of any country. Whether Amin was trying to stabilize his position by reaching out to the United States or whether this was an attempt to frighten Moscow into working with him, it backfired with the most dire consequence.

STATESMAN 1 I honestly don't know what he wanted.

STATESMAN 2 The tea was good though.

LIGHTS UP ON MOSCOW.

USTINOV IS TALKING TO A HALF-STONED BREZHNEV.

BREZHNEV   Why is he meeting with the CIA?

USTINOV   Comrade Secretary, we do not know why he was meeting with the CIA!

BREZHNEV   He is a CIA agent! Who else would he be meeting with?

USTINOV   Comrade Secretary, the CIA thing was all us. There is no…

BREZHNEV   Of course he is CIA! Why else would he be meeting with them?!

USTINOV   Comrade Secretary, these were diplomats…

BREZHNEV   They were CIA! You have let a CIA operative take over control of Afghanistan!

USTINOV   Comrade Andropov…

LIGHTS DOWN ON MOSCOW.

LIGHTS UP ON THE WHITE HOUSE.

STATESMEN 1 AND 2 ARE MEETING WITH BREZHNEV AND THE DIRECTOR OF THE CIA.

STATESMAN 1 We honestly don't know what wants!

DIRECTOR   He's definitely not one of ours.

BRZEZINSKI   You're sure of that?

DIRECTOR   Look, I don't even think an approach was made. What the hell did we want with someone like that, anyway?

BRZEZINSKI LOOKS AWAY IN SCORN.

BRZEZINSKI   And you don't know what he wanted?

STATESMAN 1 He just talked state.

STATESMAN 2 I liked the tea!

LIGHTS UP ON MOSCOW.

LIGHTS DOWN ON THE WHITE HOUSE.

ANDROPOV   Don't be ridiculous!

USTINOV   Then why is he meeting with the Americans?

ANDROPOV   Maybe he likes… I don't know why he's meeting with the Americans.

USTINOV   He could be though. CIA.

ANDROPOV   What? The counter intelligence we put out to discredit the ruler we seek to assassinate is actual intelligence that is leading to the Americans trying to set up a dummy republic? You are watching too much TV.

USTINOV   It could be!

LIGHTS UP ON THE WHITE HOUSE AND AMIN.

DIRECTOR   He's not.

ANDROPOV   Don't be absurd.

BRZEZINSKI   Don, he'd better not be, that's what I'm telling you.

USTINOV   He'd better not be, Comrade, because this whole CIA idea…

BRZEZINSKI   Because if I find out that the CIA are running covert ops around this White House…

ANDROPOV   Have care with your tongue Comrade. It is not wise to threaten the sitting head of the KGB.

DIRECTOR   Categorically, he's not, I repeat…

ANDROPOV   …not, CIA. Understand?

BRZEZINSKI   If you say so.

ANDROPOV   Be sure to tell the Comrade Secretary. Or better yet, tell his nurse.

EXIT ALL BUT ANDROPOV, BRZEZINSKI, AND AMIN.

AMIN   I'm not. And I wasn't. CIA. But then I wasn't KGB either.

BRZEZINSKI   This could be the very thing that sends them over the edge.

ANDROPOV   (INTO THE PHONE) Find Babrak Karmal and find him now!

SCENE 12

AFGHANISTAN.

ENTER MOTHER CARRYING A SUITCASE.

MOTHER   Son. (THERE IS NO ANSWER) Son!

ENTER BOY.

HE IS DRESSED IN PYJAMAS. CLEARLY HE'S BEEN ASLEEP.

BOY   Maadar.

MOTHER   (HANDING HIM A SUITCASE) Get dressed. Pack your things.

BOY   Maadar?

MOTHER   Pack your things. We're leaving.

BOY   Where.

MOTHER   Get dressed. (PAUSE) They've taken your father. Get dressed.

THE BOY LOOKS AT HER THEN EXITS.

EXIT BOY.

MOTHER PUTS ON A COAT AND LOOKS AROUND FOR ANY LAST THINGS.

MOTHER   There's a bus. We'll take the bus to Jalalabad and then into Peshawar. We'll be safe there. (TO BOY) Get your things!

ENTER BOY.

BOY RE-ENTERS, PULLING ON A SHIRT. HIS MOTHER HELPS HIM.

BOY   What about father? Who took him?

MOTHER   The soldiers. At the factory. They 'liberated' the factory. We have to go. Now.

BOY   I don't want to go.

MOTHER   Think of it like a trip, yes? An exciting trip. A new place, yes? Think of it like that.

BOY   How will he find us?

MOTHER   He will find us.

BOY   How?

MOTHER   Look at me son. He is your father. He will find us. Do you understand? (THE BOY HAS FINISHED DRESSING) Now, let's go.

EXIT BOY AND MOTHER.

SCENE 13

MOSCOW.

BREZHNEV, ANDROPOV, USTINOV, AND GROMYKO ARE SITTING AROUND A TABLE, TALKING UP PLANS FOR THE INVASION.

BREZHNEV'S NURSE IS FUSSING AROUND HIM AND HE SWATS AT HER LIKE A FLY.

QUIETLY AT FIRST, BUT CONSISTENT AND GROWING IN VOLUME DURING THE SCENE, THE SOUND OF A TANK CAN BE HEARD.

NURSE (TA)   By December 1979 it was clear to the Soviet Union that it was going to have to either invade or risk losing Afghanistan, possibly to the Americans. A meeting of the chiefs was called. Present were Secretary General Brezhnev and head of the KGB Yuri Andropov, as well as chief advisors Ustinov and Gromyko.

BREZHNEV   It's settled then. (TO NURSE) Leave that alone.

USTINOV   Comrades?

ANDROPOV   It's settled.

GROMYKO   America cannot take Afghanistan. If it does, it can place short-range missiles in there in weeks. The entire southern block could…

BREZHNEV   Yes, yes.

USTINOV   It would be Cuba all over again. (BEAT) Only the other way round.

ANDROPOV   Comrade Gromyko. How do we proceed?

GROMYKO   We already have two divisions in place near Amin. Ostensibly there to protect him, but…

ANDROPOV   Talk to me about the army first.

GROMYKO   We place a battalion at Kabul airport…

USTINOV   Quietly.

GROMYKO   Quietly; and another three at Bagram. We then move the Turmenistan and C.A.M.D. across the border. Then we drop the 105th into Kabul and surround the city completely.

ANDROPOV   How long will that take?

GROMYKO   Two days. Another two to secure the city.

BREZHNEV   Resistance?

GROMYKO   We've already started to remove many of the army's tanks and airplanes under the guise of maintenance.

USTINOV   And they fell for that?

GROMYKO   What do they know? Anyway, the point is that resistance will be minimal.

ANDROPOV   From the army.

GROMYKO   From the army.

BREZHNEV   Which brings us to Amin. How do we replace him.

ANDROPOV   A plan has already been set in motion.

LIGHTS UP ON AMIN.

AMIN AND HIS FAMILY ARE HAVING DINNER, EATING AND TALKING AND THOUGH THERE IS AN AIR OF TENSION AROUND THE TABLE THE TALK – SILENT TO US – SEEMS JOVIAL.

AMIN IS NOT EATING MUCH.

USTINOV   Seven hundred KGB agents, dressed as Afghan troops, will move across the border and take control of the palace

ANDROPOV   It is imperative, however, that Amin is not killed. This was the problem last time. We keep killing faction leaders and soon there will be no more communists in Afghanistan.

USTINOV   Besides, we want to know how much he knows about the CIA.

ANDROPOV ROLLS HIS EYES.

A WAITER ENTERS AND POURS DRINKS FOR THE FAMILY.

ANDROPOV   An agent has already been put in place in the palace. Once we are in range, he will deliver a sleeping drug to the entire family…

BREZHNEV   How?

ANDROPOV   Through the food probably. We will then smuggle them out into the Soviet Union and give Amin a choice. Work with Karmal or be shot. He will work with Karmal.

GROMYKO   Mr. Secretary. This cloak and dagger nonsense…

USTINOV   It will work.

GROMYKO   That is what the Americans said about Tehran.

ANDROPOV   It will work.

DURING THIS TALK THE FAMILY HAS FALLEN INTO A DRUG INDUCED SLEEP AT THE TABLE.

GUNFIRE AND SHOUTING CAN BE HEARD FROM OFF STAGE RIGHT.

BREZHNEV   And Camel?

USTINOV   Karmal.

ANDROPOV   Karmal will be in place by the new year. He will claim he returned triumphantly from exile to lead the Afghan army in a revolt and has taken control of the country, with or without Amin. He will then claim he asked for Soviet aid in routing out the insurrectionists and… whatever we decide to call them. We will have broken no international laws and we will have control of the country.

SOLDIERS RUN INTO THE DINING ROOM BUT AMIN HAS BEEN AWAKENED BY THE NOISE. HE PULLS A GUN ON THE SOLDIERS WHO FIRE ON HIM, KILLING HIM. THEY THEN FIRE ON THE FAMILY.

THE TANK NOISE IS NOW VERY LOUD.

GROMYKO   As long as nothing goes wrong.

ANDROPOV   Nothing will go wrong.

BREZHNEV   Before the Olympics.

USTINOV   Nothing will go wrong.

BREZHNEV   I'm tired. Nurse?

THE NURSE HELPS HIM RETIRE. THE OTHERS STAND TO EXIT.

GROMYKO   If we go in there without legitimacy we'll be invading a sovereign nation.

ANDROPOV   Nothing will go wrong.

THE NOISE OF THE TANK IS NOW A DEAFENING ROAR.

LIGHTS BEAM OUT INTO THE AUDIENCE, BLINDING THEM.

END OF ACT ONE.

ACT TWO

ACT TWO

SCENE 1

THE NOISE FROM THE TANK STARTS TO FADE INTO THE NOISE OF A FIGHTER JET TAKING OFF.

LIGHTS FROM THE TANK START TO RISE AS IF IN TAKE-OFF. THE LIGHTS DISAPPEAR INTO THE GANTRY OF THE STAGE AND THE SOUND OF THE JET DISAPPEARS OVER THE HEADS OF THE AUDIENCE.

A SOVIET FIGHTER PILOT WALKS OUT ONTO THE STAGE, HIS HELMET UNDER ONE ARM, LIGHTING A CIGARETTE.

A GROUND CREWMAN RUNS OUT AFTER HIM, HOLDING OUT A CLIPBOARD WHICH THE PILOT TAKES.

CREWMAN   Comrade.

PILOT   Did you take a look at the back wheel?

CREWMAN   Bird sheer.

PILOT   Yeah?

CREWMAN   Same problem all week. The air is thick with birds this time of year. We've been picking carcasses out all day.

PILOT   As long as that is not what they're serving tonight. (HE LOOKS AT THE BOARD AND THEN HANDS IT BACK) Spaciba. This heat is killing me.

CREWMAN   (MOTIONING TO THE CIGARETTES) Russian?

PILOT   Czech.

CREWMAN   Comrade?

THE PILOT SIGHS AND HANDS ONE OVER.

PILOT   When am I up again?

CREWMAN   Three hours.

PILOT   Bozhe moi.

CREWMAN   How many flights does that make it?

PILOT   In these two days? Nine.

CREWMAN   You're…

PILOT   Air cover. Though what for I have no idea. We've landed 100,000 troops in the last twenty-four hours. 100,000 and not one incident.

CREWMAN   There's more flights scheduled throughout the night. The bombers…

PILOT   Yeah.

CREWMAN   How long do you think? We'll be here; how long?

PILOT   In Afghanistan?

CREWMAN   How long do you think we'll be here?

PILOT   This is part of the Soviet Union now. Forever.

CREWMAN   I mean the troops.

PILOT   Three months. A year at most.

CREWMAN   That's what I think. You know what I think? I think we'll be out of here in six months. These backward,,, I don't even know why we want them? What does the Soviet Union want with a mountain country anyway? We don't have enough mountains in Russia?

PILOT   Aren't there suppose to be…

CREWMAN   Comrade?

PILOT   Aren't there supposed to be guards. At the end of the runway?

CREWMAN   It's… They must be between shifts?

PILOT   Go ask someone, yes? We would not want our fighters to have more problems than birds.

CREWMAN   Comrade.

EXIT CREWMAN.

THE PILOT LIGHTS ANOTHER CIGARETTE. HE SPIES A LARGE BAG AT THE END OF THE RUNWAY, ROUGH AND DARK. LOOKING AROUND HE APPROACHES IT SLOWLY, KICKS IT, THEN, CHECKING TO SEE IF ANYONE IS AROUND, BENDS AND OPENS IT.

THE ARMS AND LEGS OF SOLDIERS IN SOVIET UNIFORMS FALL OUT. THE PILOT TURNS AND RUNS OFF-STAGE.

THE LIGHTS FALL.

A CACOPHONY OF VOICES IN PRAYER SOUND OUT OF THE STAGE, A MUSLIM CHANT AS ANGRY AND FRIGHTENING AS IT IS BEAUTIFUL.

HART (TA)   During the first night of the occupation in Kabul, a thousand voices cry out in prayer. The longest, most costly, and most international jihad that the world has ever known has started. India, China, Egypt, Iran, Saudi Arabia, Israel, the United Kingdom, Pakistan, and the United States will all play their part in the decade long struggle against Soviet invasion (BEAT) uniting Muslim and Christian, bridging international hatred and distrust and killing over a million Afghans in the process.

Never, in the history of the world, has so large and so expansive a secret operation ever been undertaken.

SCENE 2

AFGHANISTAN.

HART IS STANDING IN THE MIDDLE OF THE MIDDLE OF THE NIGHT, SMOKING. TWO MUJAHIDEENS ARE GUARDING HIM, LAZILY.

THE SOUND OF A MOTORBIKE DRAWS THEIR ATTENTION AND NERVOUSLY HART STUBS OUT THE CIGARETTE.

A MOTORBIKE ENTERS ONSTAGE, CARRYING HAQ DRESSED IN A SOVIET PILOT'S UNIFORM.

HART IS NERVOUS, BUT HIS GUARDS ARE NONPLUSSED.

HAQ DISMOUNTS.

HAQ   You are CIA? (HART DOESN'T ANSWER. HAQ SPEAKS TO THE GUARDS IN PERSIAN) Ingilisi harf nemizaneh? (TO HART) You are the CIA man, yes?

HART   Who the fuck are you?

HAQ   The uniform? You like it? It is a Soviet pilot. Good for the cold.

HART   Haq?

HAQ   I am Abdul Haq. You are the CIA man?

HART   Hart.

HAQ   Like the kidney?

HART   If you like.

HAQ   Welcome to Afghanistan!

HART   You scared the shit out of me.

HAQ   (TO GUARDS) Boro. Did you have any problems? (HART SHAKES HIS HEAD) Good. (BEAT) It is a pity we meet at night.

EXIT GUARDS.

HART   I'm already breaking… If the Soviets find out I'm here… What I'm doing here is an act of war. I mean, not 'it might be'; it is. The Soviets find out I'm here and it's game over.

HAQ   I mean it is a shame you come at night because you cannot see my beautiful country. That valley. You just came through? That is the Khyber Pass. Just there. It is very beautiful.

HART   I'll have to take your word for it.

HAQ   You wanted to see me?

HART   Yeah. As you know, we, the CIA, have been dealing with the ISI…

HAQ   Akhtar.

HART   Exactly.

HAQ   The man is crazy. Good crazy, don't get me wrong. A great warrior, but crazy.

HART   This from a man riding a motorcycle dressed like a Soviet pilot.

HAQ   From a man risking nuclear war between two superpowers to meet a motorbike in the mountains.

HART   As I say, we've been dealing with the ISI.

HAQ   And you're worried that the arms aren't getting where they need to go.

HART   We're worried about a lot of things.

HAQ   They're not.

HART   (PAUSE) The Mujahideen…

HAQ   Look at this (HE PICKS UP A STICK AND BEGINS TO DRAW ON THE GROUND) This is my country. And this, this is you, tonight. This is us. And this. (HE STARTS TO SHADE THE COUNTRY IN) This is what you call the Mujahideen. Here. All of it. From Massoud and Rabbani in the north to Karzai in the south. All of it. But this. (HE PUTS A DOT ON THE MAP) Is where the arms are going. Look at me. I drive a Soviet motorcycle. I wear a Soviet pilot's uniform. Do you think the CIA made these? Do you think they came from India? The ISI are funding the jihad here. Yes, some weapons make it through to others. The Northern Alliance, the Muslim Brotherhood, but these are few and far between. The ISI do not like to share.

HART   Hekmatyar…

HAQ   Hekmatyar is in the work of the ISI. The ISI is in the work of Pakistan. The weapons you are sending us are made in China and Saudi Arabia, Egypt. Do you think any of these countries have the good of the Afghan people in mind?

HART   Zia…

HAQ   Zia does not control the ISI. The ISI does not control the ISI. This war… let me ask you… this war… Does the United States… Do you want to free Afghanistan or do you want to kill Soviet troops?

HART   We want to up the stakes.

HAQ   I'm listening.

HART   Three things. First; you're damn right, we want to kill

Soviets. So, here's the thing. Any warlord, any warlord who brings back the belt buckle of a Soviet soldier's going to get a reward. That's one. It's what the Soviets used to do for us in Vietnam so it's what we're doing here.

HAQ   How much?

HART   Whatever we damn well say.

HAQ   Go on.

HART   Two. This.

HART FLINGS A COPY OF THE QURAN AT HAQ WHO CATCHES AND READS IT.

HAQ   A Quran?

HART   We want your help spreading them. Not just in Afghanistan, we want to use your connections with the transport guys to get them into the Soviet Block. Tajikistan, Uzbekistan… Wherever they'll do most good.

HAQ   Muslims kill Russians.

HART   Exactly. If we can get what's happening here in Afghanistan to happen in other places…

HAQ   What's the third thing?

HART   The CIA wishes to deal directly with the Mujahideen. You're right about the ISI. They've got their own game and it's not necessarily ours. Who do we deal with?

HAQ   You're talking weapons?

HART   Weapons, explosives, food, gas, money. Who do we talk to?

HAQ   You are talking to him.

HART   Who do we talk to?

HAQ   Massoud, Abdul, Khan. These are all good men. Men of influence.

HART   You can talk to them?

HAQ   With enough time.

HART   What you asked me before?

HAQ   Yes?

HART   Whether the CIA wanted to kill Soviets or free Afghanistan?

HAQ   Yes.

HART   We want to do both.

HAQ   Then I think we have a friendship.

HART   One more thing.

HAQ   Yes.

HART   Don't ever come to me again in a Soviet uniform. Muslims aren't the only people who like to kill Soviets, if you know what I mean.

HAQ   I like you. Together we will free Afghanistan.

HART   Imagine my joy.

HAQ MOUNTS HIS MOTORCYCLE AND EXITS. HART TURNS TO THE GUARDS.

HART   Right. Back we go then. And let's try not to hit so many damn potholes on the way this time, shall we?

EXIT HART AND THE GUARDS.

SCENE 3

WE HEAR A JET LANDING. SAUDI DELEGATES RUSH UP TO MEET IT.

CASEY AND AN AIDE STEP OFF THE PLANE.

DELEGATE 1   Mr. Casey.

AIDE   Director Casey.

DELEGATE 1   Yes, of course. Prince Turki is waiting for you.

EXIT DELEGATE 1 AND CASEY.

THE AIDE TAKES DELEGATE 2 ASIDE.

AIDE   Listen, I'm… The Director is, well, how should we

say it. He's a religious man. And it's a Sunday.

DELEGATE 2   Yes?

AIDE   He'd… appreciate… attending a service.

DELEGATE 2   A Christian service?

AIDE   A Catholic service.

DELEGATE 2   Mrs…

AIDE   Miss.

DELEGATE 2   Saudi Arabia is a…

AIDE   Monotheistic country. I know.

DELEGATE 2   I do not know this word, is it onomatopoeic?

AIDE   I… No… It means…

DELEGATE 2   The practice of all other religions has been banned in Saudi Arabia. It is against the law.

AIDE   Still. The director would… appreciate it.

EXIT AIDE AND DELEGATE 2.

ENTER CASEY AND PRINCE TURKI.

PRINCE   Mr. Casey, I can assure you. We share your plight for our brothers in Afghanistan.

CASEY   This is a religious war, Prince Turki. It is the side of God against the godless. I can assure you that Afghanistan has no bigger supporter than the White House. President Reagan.

PRINCE   President Carter…

CASEY   President Reagan is not President Carter.

PRINCE   Nevertheless…

CASEY   We've got a German publishing company printing copies of the Quran in Uzbeki, for crying out loud. Uzbeki! We're in this to win. We want to help the freedom fighters of Afghanistan and we want you to help us help them.

PRINCE   We have members of the GID fighting alongside the freedom fighters. We have members of the royal family in the region helping to build roads. The roads…

CASEY   Are too thin. I know all this. Chinese cutters aren't cutting it. The Mujas can't travel fast enough.

PRINCE   Mujahideens. We know all this. It is, in fact, a surprise to us that America thinks we do not know this.

CASEY   What we lack in cunning we make up for in guile.

PRINCE   Mr. Casey.

CASEY   Director Casey, though it couldn't matter less.

PRINCE   …matter less, Prince Turki. And it couldn't matter more.

CASEY   Listen. Prince. Without the rocket launchers the game's over. They need the guns, Prince. We… Now we've upped our stake in this thing to the tune of nearly two hundred million a year. That's in just a couple of years, you know what I'm saying? We want to win this thing and, listen…

PRINCE   Prince Turki.

CASEY   Listen. Your Highness. This whole thing folds, and where do you think they're coming to? You think the Soviets want Afghanistan? You think it's anything more than a mountain pass to them right now? This is where the oil is. This is a warm water port, you hear what I'm saying? Can you help us out?

PRINCE   (SIGHS) You shall have our support. Of course. You are meeting with President Zia?

CASEY   Flying out right after.

PRINCE   Ah, yes.

CASEY   Now, if you'll excuse me, I think your boys have managed to find the last Catholic priest in the Kingdom to do a mass for me and my boys.

EXIT CASEY. ENTER DELEGATE 3.

DELEGATE 3   Who was that?

PRINCE   That? That is the head of America's CIA.

DELEGATE 3   I thought it was John Wayne.

PRINCE   John Wayne is dead. (SOTTO) And taking mass in the royal palace.

SCENE 4

MASSOUD STANDS CENTRE STAGE. HE IS YOUNG,
SLIGHTLY UNCOMFORTABLE, BUT CONFIDENT.

MASSOUD   My friends. (PAUSE) And we are all friends
here. Though we hardly know each other. Though we know next
to nothing about each other. We are friends. We are Pashtuns, we
are Hazara. We are Persians (BEAT) and we are pirates. But we are
friends. Friends of this country, friends of the lands that our fathers
tilled, friends of the rain that watered the crops. We are friends of the
mountain snow and we are friends of the valley heat. Friends of the
marketplace and of the evening prayers. We are friends, and we are
brothers. And we are welcome.

The Soviets have decided to claim this friendship as their own. They
have come in many ways, they have come by the back door, they
have come overland and they have come by air. But they have never
once come with respect. Never once with the thought of the people
in their minds and never once without bloodshed. They (BEAT) are
not.

I have spent my whole life preparing for war and praying to Allah that
my training would be in vain. For some of us that is not true. This is
not a war that will be won in a day. I will train you, on this you have
my word. You have my promise. You will learn tactics, you will learn
intelligence, you will learn to fight, and then, and only then, will the
Soviets learn to fear us.

The Soviet army has taken over many countries, this will be their
last. The Soviet army has never, in the last forty years, never lost even
one of the countries they invaded, but I swear this to you, now, before
my friends and before Allah, may his name endure, they will lose this
one. Before us and before this friendship, this country, this people,
they will lose this land. They will lose it, and they will regret ever
coming here, or I will lose my blood to these rocks, to this friendship,
and to the glory of Afghanistan.

BLACKOUT.

SCENE 5

PAKISTAN.

CASEY'S JET LANDS. THIS TIME HART IS THERE TO MEET HIM ALONG WITH AKHTAR.

THE AIDE ENTERS FOLLOWED BY CASEY.

CASEY Howard.

HART   Bill. (HANDING HIM A FLASK) Here. You'll need this.

CASEY What is it?

HART   Whisky. Zia keeps a dry palace.

CASEY And the search for civilization continues. What's with Rocky over there?

HART   Director Casey, may I introduce Director Akhtar of the ISI, the Pakistan intelligence service.

CASEY Good to meet you.

AKHTAR Likewise.

ENTER PRESIDENT ZIA.

ZIA   Now I have three warriors to look after, is it?

HART   Director Casey…

CASEY President Zia. We meet at last.

ZIA   Mr. Casey. Please. Have a seat. Can I get you some refreshment? Tea, perhaps?

CASEY Ah, no.

ZIA   If you are tired from your trip…

CASEY Listen, Mr. President…

ZIA   You have some questions.

CASEY I do. Yes.

ZIA   Do you know, perhaps? Why we called it Pakistan?

CASEY I don't. No.

ZIA   That is a pity. But anyway. The questions.

CASEY Right. Yes. Listen, President Zia. I've just come from a meeting with the Saudi prince.

ZIA   I trust he is well.

CASEY As a fiddle. And he's agreed to help back the arms you needed.

ZIA   The A90s?

CASEY And the government of the US has agreed to sell you the planes you asked for.

ZIA   With the guidance?

CASEY The full three billion.

ZIA   (LOOKING AT AKHTAR) This is good news.

CASEY We also… Howard likes what you're doing along the border. The training camps. The schools…

ZIA   Madrassas. One million refugees, Mr. Casey. In the first year alone. Soon there will be three. These are families, you understand? Families in tents. With no money and nowhere to go.

CASEY And we're aware of the situation. But we, Howard, we like what you're doing with the camps. The training. These boys are ready to go out and fight and all they need is the equipment to do it. That's what we're looking to give them.

ZIA   Thank you. You had some questions?

CASEY Who's this Massoud?

AKHTAR AND ZIA LOOK AT EACH OTHER.

ZIA   I'm not sure I follow?

CASEY Mass–UD. According to our boys in Langley he's the most successful fighter we… Where's those stats?

THE AIDE HANDS HIM A PIECE OF PAPER.

CASEY (CONT.) Fourteen thousand tanks… Yeah, okay, this is the wrong paper. (HE HANDS IT BACK TO THE AIDE) But if I had the right piece of paper it would tell you that this guy's guys are doing more in the Soviet's own backyard right now than anyone else and what's more, they're fighting with Hekmatyar's guys. You know that?

ZIA   These men are bandits. Nothing more. They rape the countryside…

CASEY They kill Soviets.

ZIA   The ISI must oversee distribution…

CASEY The Brit's tell me…

ZIA   Forgive me Mr. Casey, but I am not used to being interrupted in my own home.

CASEY Forgive me, Mr. President.

ZIA   Go on.

CASEY MI6. MI6 and the French. They're in and out of there all the time. We've got RU220. But they don't.

ZIA   I don't…

CASEY They're meeting with this Massoud. With this… What do they call him?

HART   The Lion of Panjshir.

CASEY The Lion of Panjshir. And they say he's the real deal.

ZIA   I see. You must understand, Mr. Casey. You must understand that Pakistan is the country that is under threat from Soviet invasion. Not Britain and not France. Pakistan. We are fighting a war for our very existence. So please, do not tell us who to deal with and who not to. Please.

AKHTAR It's insulting.

THE CIA MEN LOOK AT EACH OTHER.

ZIA   You would like to see the camps?

CASEY The training camps?

ZIA   This can be arranged.

CASEY I'd like that very much.

ZIA   Director Akhtar will take you up. Mr. Hart. Always nice to see you.

HART   Mr. President.

THE THREE SHAKE HANDS. HART AND CASEY MOVE TO ANOTHER PART OF THE STAGE.

ZIA   The training base is set up.

AKHTAR We moved them out there yesterday.

CASEY You trust these guys?

HART   Zia says jump, Akhtar gets a spring board.

ZIA   He will not know the difference?

AKHTAR No.

CASEY The money should come through to station within the week.

ZIA   These men; sometimes…. The Director of the CIA wants to run around a guerilla training camp in Pakistan. I ask you. Please, seriously, I ask you, try not to get him shot, yes?

HART   What's the plan?

CASEY The plan? You're a young man; here's your bag of money, go raise hell. Don't fuck it up. Just go out there and kill Soviets, take care of the Pakistanis and make them do whatever you need to make them do it.

AKHTAR Mr. President.

HART   Simple enough.

LIGHTS DOWN ON ZIA AND AKHTAR.

CASEY You've seen these camps?

HART   You're in for a treat.

SCENE 6

REFUGEE CAMPS IN PAKISTAN.

THE REFUGEES MILL AROUND.

HART (TA)   During the nineteen eighties, over five million Afghans, one third of the country, leave. Some move west, towards Iran, Europe, and America, but for most there is no escape from the camps in Pakistan.

Those who are able to work. Some build mud huts. Others survive in tents. Medical supplies are low. Food is scarce. There is no entertainment and no purpose. With their fathers fighting inside the country many families are forced to support themselves. Conditions are squalid. Women are forced to beg, children study in ISI founded and CIA sponsored Madrassas learning nothing except jihad and rudimentary teachings. Preparing for war against the godless Soviet invaders.

THE CROWD PARTS TO SHOW CHILDREN LEARNING IN A MADRASSAS AND THEN COME TOGETHER AGAIN.

HART (TA, CONT.)   The camp becomes a regular visiting place for journalists and dignitaries. Texas Congressman and champion of the Mujahideen plight, Charlie Wilson, is a regular visitor. Often with friends.

THE CROWD PARTS TO SHOW WILSON AND MISS NORTHERN HEMISPHERE, SNOWFLAKE.

WILSON   These boys are ready to fight. All they need are Stingers to do it.

SNOWFLAKE   It's a real eye opener, jus' being here. A real eye opener.

THE CROWD COVERS THEM AGAIN.

HART (TA)   For the Afghans themselves however, life is far from pleasant.

WE HEAR THE NOISE OF A HELICOPTER COMING IN STAGE LEFT. THE CROWD, PANICKED, STARTS TO FLEE.

HART (TA, CONT.)   Soviet helicopters make night raids into Pakistan, coming up behind the Mujahideen as they travel back into their country.

BULLETS CUT DOWN THE FLEEING CROWDS. WE HEAR THE SOUND OF A PLANE, STAGE RIGHT, FOLLOWED BY A SONIC BOOM.

HART (TA, CONT.)   Planes create sonic booms over mountain passes to start avalanches.

THE STAGE IS CLEARED EXCEPT FOR A SMALL CHILD, LIT CENTRE STAGE. THE CHILD SEES A CANDY A FEW FEET AHEAD AND REACHES OUT FOR IT. THE CHILD'S MOTHER RUSHES ONSTAGE, PANICKED.

MOTHER   No!!!

THE CHILD PICKS UP THE SWEET AND A MINE IS LAUNCHED INTO THE AIR. IT HOVERS FOR A SECOND, THE CHILD WATCHING IT, THE MOTHER REACHING THE CHILD, AND THEN IT EXPLODES IN A FLASH OF LIGHT.

BLACKOUT.

HART (TA)   Over ten million mines are placed throughout the country, many aimed at children, designed to debilitate families, and disfiguring an entire generation of Afghans. No family is without loss. No child untouched by war.

In the ten years of fighting against the Soviets, nearly twenty percent of Afghans are killed or injured.

SCENE 7

FAKE TRAINING CAMP IN PAKISTAN.

FIVE MEN WITH RIFLES, OSTENSIBLY AFGHANS, ENTER AND LINE UP IN FRONT OF THE AUDIENCE. A SIXTH, THEIR COMMANDER, ENTERS TO THE SIDE, HOLDING A SWORD. HE RAISES IT AND THEY COCK THEIR WEAPONS AND POINT THEM AT THE AUDIENCE.

COMMANDER Fire!

THEY FIRE AND RELOAD.

BEHIND THEM, ANOTHER INSTRUCTOR RUNS A NUMBER OF INFANTRY THROUGH DISARMING TECHNIQUES, AND A THIRD INSTRUCTOR TEACHES WARFARE TECHNIQUES TO A CLASS OFF STAGE.

ALL OF THEM ARE NOISY AND BOISTEROUS.

ENTER CASEY, AKHTAR, AND GUARDS.

CASEY IS BLINDFOLDED.

CASEY This really necessary?

AKHTAR Security is paramount.

THEY REMOVE THE BLINDFOLD AND CASEY LOOKS OUT OVER THE SCENE, ENTRANCED.

CASEY How many boys you got here?

AKHTAR Three hundred. At the moment.

CASEY (IMPRESSED) Three hundred!

AKHTAR We keep it small. That way the Soviets cannot attack them all.

CASEY They working this far south?

AKHTAR By plane.

CASEY How many in total. Mujas?

AKHTAR Mujahideens. I would say a hundred thousand. Maybe two. It is difficult to tell. They are not all under ISI control.

CASEY Right.

AKHTAR They cross by night. Each commander, the ones under ISI control, they have the intel you give us. Mr. Hart is good with giving us photos, from your satellites. They cross at night, through the pass.

CASEY Up the Khyber.

AKHTAR Maybe they are gone a week, maybe a month, maybe three. Their families are here, in the camps. They come here, we train them, we give them new weapons, the C4 you gave us…

CASEY Why aren't the bridges going down? The whole point of the C4 was to blow up the bridges, cripple the Soviets' pathways.

AKHTAR The Afghans do not think like that.

CASEY What do you mean?

AKHTAR If they, how did you say, 'cripple' the Soviets, they cripple their own people as well. Food must travel to the cities. Farmers must make their livings. They are simple that way. If the Soviets cannot travel, the people cannot travel. It is as simple as that.

CASEY And the bombings?

AKHTAR Afghans will not do suicide runs. This makes it difficult. They want their country free, not dead. We will train them.

CASEY Listen, the Soviets… It's not enough to make them pay, you understand? For every dollar we're putting into this they're putting ten, and that's great. Ten thousand Mujas but over one hundred thousand Soviets. Eventually they're going to wear them down. They have to take out the high commands. They have to make it costly not just in numbers, or money, but in people. Important people!

AKHTAR I will pass this along.

CASEY Now, tell me about the A90s. How you gonna train them.

AKHTAR First you train us, then we train them.

CASEY Wouldn't it just be easier to get our guys to train them?

AKHTAR Perhaps. But the question then would be; why are you all in Pakistan?

CASEY I see.

AKHTAR Kabul must burn!

SCENE 8

ALL BUT ONE OF THE GUNMEN HAVE LEFT THE STAGE. THE LAST, UNSTEADY AND UNABLE TO RELOAD, STAYS CENTRE STAGE.

MASSOUD APPEARS BEHIND HIM AND APPROACHES, HANDING HIM AN OIL CAN.

MASSOUD   Use the oil.

THE YOUNG SOLDIER TURNS AT HIS VOICE, HIS NERVES DOUBLING.

MASSOUD   You must keep your gun well oiled. Clean and well oiled. Metal expands in heat, bullets sweat. Use the oil. Not too much. A good weapon will kill your enemy. A bad one is more likely to kill you.

THE SOLDIER DOES SO AND THE BULLET SLIDES IN.

MASSOUD   There. See. Now aim… lower than that. From the shoulder. A gun is your arm: see? It is an extension of your shoulder. Think of the barrel as your wrist, the end as your finger. Now point. (THE BOY FIRES) Better.

SAAYA   Commander Massoud

MASSOUD   (TO THE BOY) Now. Go. Practice. (TO SAAYA) What do they say?

SAAYA   Ten thousand. At the least. That last convoy we hit…

MASSOUD SIGHS AND WALKS AWAY, THINKING.

SAAYA   We should make a break. For the border.

MASSOUD   Which one?

SAAYA   Does it matter?

MASSOUD   What is their level of optimism?

SAAYA   Amer Saleb?

MASSOUD   How many troops do they expect to lose?

SAAYA   Half. Uzbeks.

MASSOUD   Uzbeks.

SAAYA   We should stay. Fight.

MASSOUD   And then what?

SAAYA   What we always do. Win!

MASSOUD   With how many of us left. No, we have no food. Little real ammo. The explosives are nearly gone and we cannot leave the valley anymore than they can let us stay here.

ENTER ANDROPOV AND AIDE.

AIDE   Comrade Secretary General?

ANDROPOV   What is it?

MASSOUD   There may be another way though. If they think they will lose that many. And even then they cannot be sure of getting us all.

AIDE   (HANDING HIM A PAPER) From Comrade Gemelkin.

MASSOUD   Also, there is legend. Is there not? Even if they kill us all. Legend. It's a powerful thing. These Leninists understand that.

ANDROPOV   Ah, Gemelkin. Just take the damn valley.

MASSOUD   Who do we have in the army? Close to the top?

SAAYA   The Soviet army?

MASSOUD   Who can get the message across that needs to be got across?

SAAYA   Gemelkin. He has the ear of the Secretary General. Or so he says.

MASSOUD   Alright. Tell him this.

ANDROPOV   A truce. Is this what it comes to? A truce with a bunch of bandits.

AIDE   We've already had Karmal deny his existence. And Kabul desperately needs supplies.

ANDROPOV   Which they are stopping.

AIDE   They've repelled six full scale attacks on the valley. Every one of our supplies…

ANDROPOV   Yes. Fine. But tell Gemelkin this; he can offer these bandits a truce. He can offer them amnesty for all I care. But quietly, and without fuss, I want them all dead within the year. I will not tolerate them rising again. Make that clear.

AIDE   Yes Comrade Secretary.

SAAYA   A truce! A superpower has made a truce with a valley! This is… We have beaten a superpower. The Americans will have to supply us now.

MASSOUD   We'll see. We'll see.

SCENE 9

CALIFORNIA.

AN ADMISSIONS OFFICER WAITS AT HER DESK.

THE BOY, NOW A REBELLIOUS TEEN, ENTERS AND SHE MOTIONS TO A SEAT.

ADMIN You do realize it's Sunday, right?

TEEN   Sorry. You got anything for me to sign?

ADMIN I mean, it's not like quitting college will wait until Monday or anything.

TEEN   Is there anything I should sign?

ADMIN (SIGHS) Fine. Look. I mean, it's your life and everything but, well, I'm required, under, you know, college regulations to give you the talk. Alright? (PATRONIZING VOICE) Pasadena College accepts that, yes, there are, at times, reasons to drop out of college. Family matters, etc, and we realize of course that people have, you know, inalienable rights and everything, but, and I can't stress this highly enough, not everyone is Bill Gates; you know what I mean? This tech thing isn't going to last and dropping out of college to go play in your parents' basement is…

TEEN   I'm not dropping out for anything like that.

ADMIN (SIGHS) Fine. Sign here. (THE TEEN SIGNS) Why are you dropping out?

TEEN   I'm going home.

ADMIN San Francisco?

TEEN   Afghanistan. I'm going to fight the Soviets.

ADMIN You… You do know there's a war over there, don't you?

TEEN   What did you think fighting meant? I was… You need me to sign all of these?

ADMIN   Top sheets, then initial each page. Housing, insurance…

TEEN   I was driving through the canyons, you know, yesterday. And, well, I've been thinking about it for a long time, and well, when you hit the coast, you know the place, just as you drop down into Malibu, and well, I saw the sunset, hitting off the ocean. This… warm red, spilling out over the land. And I just knew. I knew. Like I'd never known anything before. I was going home. You want me to sign here?

ADMIN   Just there.

TEEN   The Soviets are raping my country. They are killing my kinsfolk and I can't just sit here in California watching it happen. I have to do something. And it has to be today.

THE ADMINISTRATOR IS DUMBSTRUCK. SHE TAKES BACK THE PAPERS AND LOOKS AT THE SERIOUS TEEN, TRYING TO FIND SOMETHING TO SAY.

ADMIN   Have you thought about deferment?

SCENE 10

AFGHANISTAN.

NIGHT TIME.

ENTER MASSOUD, SAAYA, AND A PDPA CORPORAL.

SAAYA   Is it me or is it getting colder.

CORPORAL   This is the only place I felt we could meet.

MASSOUD   You're right. It is getting colder.

CORPORAL   Next door is the kitchen. They have a walk in freezer.

SAAYA   You have meat?

CORPORAL   For the troops, yes.

SAAYA   (GRINNING) Exactly.

MASSOUD   Saaya.

CORPORAL   It does not matter.

MASSOUD   We appreciate you meeting us like this, my friend.
I understand the risks.

CORPORAL   No risks. The Lion of Panjshir. You are famous.
But here only Afghans know what you look like and Afghans are not
talking. You don't even need a mask like that American TV thing.

SAAYA   Zorro?

CORPORAL   The Lone Ranger.

MASSOUD   What can we do for you, my friend?

CORPORAL   Commander Massoud, Saheb... The car.

SAAYA   Ah, the car.

MASSOUD   What about the car?

CORPORAL   The car you are driving was a present for the head
of foreign affairs in Kabul. From the Soviet government.

MASSOUD   My people have liberated it.

SAAYA   We will return the car.

MASSOUD   It is not the car.

CORPORAL   It is time again.

MASSOUD   What do you know?

CORPORAL   The truce is over. There is a raid. An air raid.

MASSOUD   When?

CORPORAL   Three days. Commander Massoud this time...
This is not an air raid for you. They are tired of you picking at them.
This is an air raid for the entire valley!

SAAYA   The valley?

CORPORAL   We have been told to move back to out of the valley
at first light. They mean to carpet bomb everything. High altitude.
Then they will send in the special division.

MASSOUD   To get at me?

CORPORAL   Everything. They plan to mine the valley. So you cannot come back.

PAUSE.

SAAYA   We must flee.

MASSOUD   We cannot.

SAAYA   If we head south, to Pakistan, join up with…

MASSOUD   We cannot. There are people. Farmers. Maybe eight thousand. More. All living in the valley.

SAAYA   We will get word to them.

CORPORAL   You cannot. If they move they will know and they will cancel the bombing. Maybe next time, not telling us.

MASSOUD   He's right. (BEAT) We have to move together. We'll have to move all of them.

SAAYA   What?

CORPORAL   What do you mean, all of them?

MASSOUD   I mean all of them. We will move them together. Over the mountain passes. The Soviets will never know. Saaya, send word to the people, everyone you can find. You too, my friend. Tell them to take nothing. Nothing that cannot be carried by one man, and tell them to meet us at the mosque after morning prayers tomorrow. Tell them: whoever is left behind will die. Whoever joins Massoud will live. Tell them quickly and tell them quietly. Tomorrow we are Moses. Tell them.

DURING THE SPEECH THE STAGE STARTS TO FILL UP WITH AFGHAN REFUGEES. THEY MILL AND CROWD ONTO THE STAGE.

MASSOUD AND THE OTHER DISAPPEAR INTO THE THICK OF THEM.

ENTER SOVIET GENERAL AND CORPORAL.

THE CORPORAL CROSSES SMARTLY TO THE CENTRE OF THE STAGE AND EXECUTES A SMART SALUTE.

CORPORAL   Comrade General. The report on the bombing.

HE HANDS HIM A PAPER.

GENERAL   Eight?

CORPORAL   Yes, Comrade General.

GENERAL   Is this a joke?

CORPORAL   No, Comrade General.

GENERAL   Four hours of bombing and eight bodies?

CORPORAL   We cannot explain it, Comrade General.

GENERAL   Did you check the mountains?

CORPORAL   Deserted, Comrade General. As were the villages
and farms.

GENERAL   I'm going to get to the bottom of this.

EXIT GENERAL AND CORPORAL.

SCENE 11

AFGHANISTAN.

THE TEEN IS BEING LED ALONG WITH ANOTHER GROUP
OVER THE MOUNTAINS AT NIGHT INTO AFGHANISTAN
BY SAAYA.

SAAYA   We rest here. Fifteen minutes. No cigarettes. No lights.

THEY ALL SIT AND SILENTLY DRINK TEA.

MILITANT 1   Are we there yet?

ALL EXCEPT SAAYA AND THE TEEN LAUGH AT THIS.

SAAYA   Quiet.

THE TEEN RUBS HIS FEET, DRINKS SOME TEA, AND
THEN RISES FROM THE GROUP AND HEADS UPSTAGE
WHERE HE IS VIOLENTLY SICK.

MILITANT 2   We should not have brought him.

MILITANT 1   He is slowing us down.

SAAYA   Listen to yourselves. This man has given up everything. Everything! To come here and fight with us. Yes, he is soft, but he will harden. What have you given up? A night in a tent with that wife of yours nagging at you.

THE OTHERS LAUGH. MILITANT 1 IS SILENT.

THE SOUND OF A PLANE FAR OFF CAN BE HEARD.

SAAYA   Shush.

THE NOISE GOES AWAY.

MASSOUD ENTERS FROM THE DARKNESS.

MASSOUD   The jackals can hear your laughing a valley away.

MILITANT 2   Commander Massoud.

MASSOUD AND SAAYA HUG BUT SAAYA LOOKS ANXIOUS.

MASSOUD   It is good to see you cousin. What did you bring me?

JUST AS THE TEEN IS STARTING TO RETURN TO THE GROUP, MILITANT 1 RISES AND POINTS HIS GUN AT MASSOUD.

MILITANT 1   Greetings from President Najibullah.

HE SHOOTS BUT MISSES COMPLETELY. MASSOUD FLINCHES AT FIRST BUT THEN STRAIGHTENS AND LOOKS AT THE FRIGHTENED MAN. EVERYONE ELSE COWERS BACK.

THE MAN IS ABOUT TO SHOOT AGAIN WHEN ONE OF THE OTHERS IN THE GROUP SHOOTS HIM DEAD.

MASSOUD TURNS TO LOOK AT SAAYA WHO STARTS TO BACK AWAY.

MASSOUD   Saaya.

THE MUJAHIDEEN SHOOTS HIM AND HE FALLS DYING. MASSOUD RUSHES TO HIS SIDE. THE OTHER MUJAHIDEENS EXIT IN TERROR.

MASSOUD   No! (TO THE DYING SAAYA) Saaya! It's alright. It's alright.

THE TEEN APPROACHES HIM.

TEEN   Commander. We must go. (THERE IS NO REPLY. SAAYA DIES) Commander. They will know our position.

MASSOUD   He was my cousin.

TEEN   He was a traitor!

MASSOUD   Then he deserved justice. This is not justice. This is…

TEEN   Commander.

EXIT TEEN.

MASSOUD   …war.

EXIT MASSOUD.

SCENE 12

PENTAGON / KREMLIN.

CONFERENCE TABLE CENTRE.

ENTER   CASEY,   BEARDEN,   VAUGHAN   FORREST, CLARRIDGE, GUST AVRAKADOS, AND FRED IKLE.

CASEY TAKES CENTRE.

CASEY Alright. This everyone? (THEY SIT) Before we get to it, everyone knows Bearden? As of tomorrow he's our new head of station in Islamabad. Bearden; Forrest, Clarridge, Avrakados you know, and Ikle.

BEARDEN   I'm never going to remember that.

CLARRIDGE   You won't have to.

CASEY Okay, I know we need to talk about 166, but before we do, how are we doing? Gust?

GUST   Okay. Well, first thing; the Soviets are wisening up. There's fake Mujahideen wandering around making contacts. Which is smart. They're also getting good at stocking up on Toyotas.

FORREST   Toyotas?

CASEY It's what we supply the Mujas with.

GUST   And they're good at stealing them. So that gives them cover. Also; right now, we estimate about 30,000 KGB guys in the country with another 100,000 or so informants, so odds are they've got someone on the inside of everything. Who can we trust? No one. Who do we kill? That's what we're here for.

CASEY Alright. Well, good news first up. We're at a billion. Half from us and half from the Saudis so money's not a problem. Now, let's talk about what is. NSDD 166. We've been giving them back channel aerial photos for a while now. Now that's on the level.

CLARRIDGE   Excuse me, but am I the only one that thinks that might be a problem?

BEARDEN   For who?

CLARRIDGE   For us.

ALL   No.

CLARRIDGE   If the Soviets shoot down an American plane over Soviet airspace...

GUST   They're too high for that.

CLARRIDGE   Yeah? What about these drops we're making? Inside the border? They're not too high for that. They shoot down a US plane and ignite World War III...

IKLE   World War III? That's not such a bad idea!

THEY ALL LAUGH.

CASEY Forrest? What's with these buffalo guns? Forrest here is an arms expert.

FORREST   The buffalo guns fire, in layman's terms, really big bullets, real far.

BEARDEN   How far?

FORREST   Two kilometres. It doesn't take a genius to figure out that you need to hit them hard, you need to hit them deep, and you need to hit their hearts and brains at the same time. This will do that.

GUST   Ducks in a barrel.

CLARRIDGE   Which brings us to the problem of one six six.

CASEY We know one six six…

CLARRIDGE   National Security Directorate one six six says…

CASEY We know what it says. Look; we're arming the Afghans, right? Every time a Muja kills a Soviet rifleman, are we engaged in assassination? This is a rough business, if we're afraid to hit the terrorists because somebody's going to yell 'assassination' it'll never stop. The terrorists will own the world!

CLARRIDGE   The US government cannot sanction assassination, is all I'm saying.

BEARDEN   We, that is, the CIA, stand by our position that once the stuff is delivered to the Paks, we lose all control over it.

FORREST   There is that thing with the KGB. If so many of them are…

CASEY Yeah. That's a tough one.

CLARRIDGE   Thirty years we've had the truce. We don't shoot at KGB. They don't shoot at CIA. You sure we want to change that?

THEY ALL THINK.

GUST   Don't give them the goggles.

CASEY What's that?

GUST   Don't give them the night goggles. Who assassinates people in the day? Take away the night goggles. Difficult to scream assassination if it's in the middle of a fire fight.

CASEY (THINKS) Anyone got a problem with that? (SILENCE) Alright then. Okay. No goggles it is. (BEAT) The C4s getting through? I don't hear of too many bridges coming down? Nobody? Okay. Now, stingers.

TWO MUJAHIDEENS ENTER, CARRYING A STINGER. SOUNDS OF A HELICOPTER CAN BE HEARD. THE PAIR POINT OUT INTO THE AUDIENCE AND THE STINGER IS

RAISED. THE OTHER LEVELS A SONY CAMCORDER.

GUST   If they can't shoot down the 'copters then that's the ball game.

CASEY We got them covered?

FORREST   China.

BEARDEN   Ain't nothing better than shooting down Soviets with Chinese bullets.

THEY ALL LAUGH.

THE MUJAHIDEEN LAUNCHES THE STINGER. THE HELICOPTER CRASHES. THE PAIR JUMP FOR JOY.

CASEY Better give them a camera too. The President likes to watch his briefings rather than read them.

BEARDEN   Got it.

EXIT MUJAHIDEENS.

CLARRIDGE   What happens to all this stuff if we pull out? That's what I want to know. The ISI are going to be the most well equipped militia in the world

BEARDEN   Never happen. It still looks as though the war might just go on indefinitely or the Soviets might even be on the verge of winning it.

GUST   We're in for the long haul.

CASEY And I agree. Alright, I think that covers everything. Gentlemen?

THEY ALL RISE AND HEAD OUT CHATTERING AS THEY DO.

ENTER GORBACHEV, AKHROMEYEV, SHEVARDNADZE, AND KRYUCHOV.

THE SOVIETS TAKE THEIR PLACE AT THE TABLE.

GORBACHEV Alright. Everyone sit. Shevardnadze has the reports.

SHEVARDNADZE HANDS OUT PAPERS.

GORBACHEV (CONT.) Sit. Sit. Afghanistan. Why are we there,

what is to be done? A million of our people have gone through the country and we are not able to explain to our people why we did not complete it. We have suffered such heavy losses! And what for? What are we going to do?

KRYUCHOV   Comrade Secretary General. The time has come to plan a withdrawal. The generals have had a year. More. Now is the time to act.

AKHROMEYEV   I agree with Comrade Kryuchov. This is not a war to win. I don't even know what winning it would look like.

SHEVARDNADZE   If we do not get out of Afghanistan, we will disgrace ourselves in all our relations.

GORBACHEV   Then we are agreed. Afghanistan is a bleeding wound. The strategic goal is to finish the war in one, maximum two years, and withdraw the troops.

AKHROMEYEV   What about the US?

SHEVARDNADZE   I agree. The US has set for itself the goal of disrupting a settlement in Afghanistan by any means.

GORBACHEV   We have not approached the United States of America in a real way! They need to be associated with the political solution. To be invited. This is the correct policy. There is an opportunity here. Edward. You have contacts inside the CIA?

SHEVARDNADZE   We have a mole.

GORBACHEV   I mean, you can talk to them.

SHEVARDNADZE   Yes, Comrade Secretary.

GORBACHEV   Do so.

SHEVARDNADZE   RISES   AND   MOVES   TO   MEET CLARRIDGE AS HE COMES ON.

ENTER CLARRIDGE.

AKHROMEYEV   And what of after?

GORBACHEV   You must speak to Najibullah. He must seek a national reconciliation.

CLARRIDGE   You look well.

SHEVARDNADZE   You do not. How is Comrade Casey?

CLARRIDGE   Dead. Brain haemorrhage.

SHEVARDNADZE   I am sorry to hear that.

GORBACHEV   This needs to be remembered. There can be no Afghanistan without Islam. There is nothing to replace it now. But if the name of the party is kept, then the word 'Islamic' needs to be included in it. Afghanistan needs to be returned to a condition which is natural for it. The Mujahideen need to be more aggressively invited into power at the grassroots.

CLARRIDGE   You called this meeting.

SHEVARDNADZE   We will leave Afghanistan. It may be in five months or a year, but it is not a question of it happening in the remote future. I say with all responsibility that a political decision to leave has been made.

CLARRIDGE   Really. And we're to take your word on that, are we?

SHEVARDNADZE   Do what you like. Trust me on this though. If we were to begin to withdraw troops while American aid continues, then this will lead to a bloody war in the country.

CLARRIDGE   (STANDING) Lucky for us then that the only 'aid' we're providing is through the Red Cross.

EXIT CLARRIDGE.

GORBACHEV   Hopefully, a year or so from now, this will all be over.

LIGHTS FALL ON THE SCENE.

SCENE 13

AFGHANISTAN.

OFF STAGE A TV IS PLAYING ITV'S 'THE WORLD AT WAR', EPISODE 13. MASSOUD IS SITTING CENTRE STAGE, CROSS-LEGGED, WATCHING THE TV.

TV   "Winston Churchill once told Stalin, the Mediterranean is the soft underbelly of the Third Reich. Churchill and the British chiefs of staff were sure that attacking German occupied Europe through Italy would help shorten the war. The Americans were not convinced, preferring to concentrate on the decisive blow across the English Channel. Only reluctantly did they agree to join their British Allies on the road to war..."

ENTER TEEN.

MASSOUD MUTES THE TV.

TEEN   Commander. You asked to see me.

MASSOUD   You know this program?

TEEN   The World at War? Yes. It's British, isn't it?

MASSOUD   Churchill was a great man. Eisenhower too, of course, but Churchill... Have you read his letters?

TEEN   No Commander.

MASSOUD   You should. They are... They remind me of Rumi. "Sentiment should not rule in war, but neither should it be overruled or ignored." How are you feeling?

TEEN   I am strong.

MASSOUD   You are recovered?

TEEN   I am ready to fight.

MASSOUD   As all young men are. Yes. But there is more to war than fighting. There is more to war than winning.

TEEN   I don't... I'm sorry, Commander, I'm not with you.

MASSOUD   The war is ending. The Soviets... Four years ago we negotiated a truce with the Soviets. The Northern Alliance. Now they are negotiating a truce with the world. I believe they will leave Afghanistan within a year.

TEEN   That is... that is great news, Commander. My congratulations.

MASSOUD   Not as good as you think. President Najibullah has offered me a place in his cabinet.

TEEN   Will you accept?

MASSOUD   No. The man is a mass murderer. But this is how it will go. There are too many factions. Too much… Young men love to fight but, there are more important things than fighting. I need you to go back to the United States.

TEEN   Commander.

MASSOUD   (HE HANDS HIM A MESSAGE) Your mother has called for you. She wants you to go home. She thinks you have done enough. I do not agree. There is much more you can do, but not here. I need a voice in the UN. I need eyes in America. After the war, there is peace, and peace can be as frightening as war. "Democracy is the worst of all political systems except for the others."

TEEN   I will try to remember that.

MASSOUD   That too was Churchill. You will go back. You will be my eyes in peace, yes?

TEEN   If that is what you wish, Commander.

MASSOUD   Then it is settled. You will go home. Now, help translate this for me. I want to know more about the Italian conquest.

SCENE 14

AFGHANISTAN / RUSSIA.

THE SOVIET COMMANDER BORIS GROMOV WALKS TOWARD US AS HE LEAVES AFGHANISTAN. HE IS GREETED BY HIS SON WHO GIVES HIM FLOWERS. A PRESS PHOTOGRAPHER TAKES HIS PICTURE.

TEEN (TA)   On February 15 1989, the last Soviet troops leave Afghanistan. It has been almost ten years since the assassination of President Amin and the Soviet invasion. Over three million Afghans have been made homeless in a war which has cost over fifty billion dollars and cost the lives of million Afghans alone.

General Boris Gromov, the Soviet commander is presented with flowers from his son as he leaves Afghanistan.

BLACKOUT.

SCENE 15

AYOUB (TA)   As one war ends, another begins. As the last of the Soviet troops leave the country, the mountains of Afghanistan give rise to another, universal war.

ENTER   ABU AYOUB, JAMEL AL FADL, ABU HAFS, ABU UBAIDAH, AND ABU MUSAB.

AYOUB   Are they here?

FADL   Just got in.

FADL (TA)   The jihad against the Soviets had united Muslims from all over the world, many of whom had taken up arms to fight against the Soviet invasion. (BEAT) But the Soviet Union was not the only country they had trouble with.

HAFS   How many of them?

FADL   Twelve. Twenty.

UBAIDAH   There will be more.

HAFS (TA)   These men were on a recruitment drive for their mentor, Abdullah Azzam.

MUSAB   Did we come up with a name yet?

HAQ   I like the 'Islamic Army.'

FADL   We were thinking of 'The Base', 'The Basis'

HAFS (TA)   And his student and financial backer, Osama bin Laden.

MUSAB   What does that translate as?

AYOUB   Al Qaeda.

BLACKOUT.

END OF ACT TWO.

ACT THREE

ACT THREE

SCENE 1

CURTAINS ON A LECTERN CENTRE STAGE. A MAP OF CENTRAL ASIA BEHIND.

ENTER MARTY MILLAR.

TAKING HIS PLACE BEHIND THE LECTERN HE BRANDISHES A UNOCAL BROCHURE.

MILLAR   Alright, if you could all take your seats? Thank you. Does everyone have their program? Everyone? If you don't have it take a look under your seats. That's right. There's a few changes to the schedule. This afternoon instead of a talk on the Middle East by Don Wickser we're going to be looking at the Texas primary. You all got that? Mark it in; I don't want you to forget.

Alright. Good. Let's get started. One of the key regions that UNOCAL is interested in is the former Soviet Bloc. You can all see this? With the exception of the Middle East there is absolutely no place better primed for development than Central Asia. Tajikistan. (POINTS) That's here, is sitting on over 30 billion barrels of crude oil. That's like Dallas, but with bigger hats. Okay. Thirty billion barrels, and it's right next to two of the most developing countries in the world: India and, more importantly, Pakistan.

Pakistan is one of the US's strongest allies at the moment, it is developing, and it wants oil. It wants it to the tune of 20 million barrels a year by the end of the century. More after that. Now, drilling rights have already been bought up, but what we at UNOCAL are planning, you can all see this in your handouts, what we at UNOCAL are planning is a pipeline from here, to here. Right through the heart of Afghanistan.

Ambitious, yes. We don't deny it but what we at UNOCAL, and you as our shareholders know, is that we're nothing if not ambitious. In the five years since the Soviet withdrawal Afghanistan has become, well, frankly, it's a mess. The government can't govern, the roads are unsafe. Well, when there are roads. Until now, the problem has been who to deal with. As you can see from this map the entire region where we planned to run the pipeline is well, let's call it fractious shall we? Who is in control changes from day to day. We can't deal with anyone because there's no way to tell if they're going to be there when we go back.

Luckily that's all changing

HE RIPS OFF A PIECE OF THE MAP TO SHOW THE AREA UNDER TALIBAN CONTROL.

AS HE SPEAKS, ACTORS BEHIND HIM PLAY OUT SCENES OF BRUTALITY FROM THE TALIBAN REGIME.

TALIBAN TROOPS GO DOOR TO DOOR, SHOOTING WHOEVER ANSWERS, THEN RAIDING THE HOUSE.

THEY DRAG OFF WOMEN FOR RAPE CAMPS.

A STICK IS INSERTED INTO THE ARMPIT OF MAN TO CHECK FOR BODY HAIR. HE IS THEN BEATEN.

A MAN IS CHECKED WITH A COKE CAN TO SEE IF HIS BEARD IS LONG ENOUGH. HE TOO IS BEATEN.

A WOMAN IS DRAGGED HOME, HER BURQA NOT REGULATION. HER HUSBAND IS BEATEN WITH METAL WHIPS.

One group has started to take hold of the area. We've been working closely with the Bhutto government, that's the new president of Pakistan, to try to get the pipeline up and running, and they speak highly of this group. They're called the… uh, Tali-ban. These are religious scholars. Tired of the lawlessness of the outer regions and the infighting of the Mujahideen. What they're doing is they're going around, and they're getting the guns. One town at a time. House to house. These are deeply religious people. People of faith. The Bhutto government believe they'll be in Kabul before the month is out, and from there it's going to be a pretty simple step to getting the country. Now, we think we can work with them. We really do. We've got some guys on the ground and I'm heading into the country myself to set up a dialogue and our representatives in Washington are looking to help them get recognized once they take over. And once we've done that we believe it's going to be a simple step to start running oil directly from here (POINTS) to here in what we think is going to be one of the most profitable enterprises UNOCAL has ever been involved in.

Questions? Yes?

AUD 1   I'm sorry, so you're saying that the pipeline is backed by the government of Pakistan?

MILLAR   We're working closely with the government. (ASKING FOR NEXT QUESTION) Yes?

AUD 2   This group, the... um...

MILLAR   Tali-ban. Yes.

AUD 2   The Taliban, they're part of the Pakistan government?

MILLAR   Not part of. No. They're... There's a lot of links between Pakistan and Afghanistan. There are nearly a million Afghan nationals living in the borderlands here. That's a heavy resource on the Pakistanis. They've got a vested interest in what happens in the country. A stable government, the return of the people. A lot of the kids from the Madrassas on the border, those are the religious schools, they're going over and helping so, yes, I'd say they have the backing of the people if nothing else.

AUD 2   But not direct government support.

MILLAR   What they're supplying are logistics. Road building in the new Taliban controlled area. A group of officials from Pakistan just travelled through the country on almost the exact same route we're planning for the pipeline, that was almost impossible just a few months ago. They've helped set up a microwave communication system for them in Kandahar. In fact, Pakistan Telecom has been working in the city since the Taliban took control. You can now dial local from Pakistan to Jalaalabad... and probably get them to reverse charges.

Yes?

AUD 3   The Taliban? What does that mean, by the way?

MILLAR   It means Talib. Seekers. Religious students.

AUD 4   So this is a bunch of religious students.

MILLAR   This is order from chaos. This is an opportunity for development, stability, and investment. Think of them like the Catholics, only with Kalashnikovs.

SCENE 2

PAKISTAN.

ENTER MULLAH RABBANI, GHAUS, AND OTHERS.

THE PAKISTANI OFFICIALS OFFER THEM A SEAT ON THE SOFA.

QAZI   Please, sit.

THE MEN SEEM UNCOMFORTABLE AND SIT ON THE SEAT CROSS-LEGGED, AS THOUGH SITTING ON THE FLOOR.

QAZI   You are dirtying the sofas.

BABAR Ahem, we are glad we could have this opportunity to talk to you.

RABBANI   As are we.

BABAR So, perhaps we should, well, start with… How can Pakistan help you?

RABBANI   We ask, we would ask, respectfully, please… The ISI funding of the Mujahideen must stop.

BABAR AND QAZI LOOK AT EACH OTHER.

QAZI   All of them?

RABBANI   These men have brought destruction to our country.

QAZI   They are the government.

RABBANI   They will hang.

BABAR All of them?

RABBANI   We will hang them all. All of them.

QAZI   (LOOKING AT BABAR) We'll, um, we'll see what we can do.

BABAR Is there anything else we can do for you?

LIGHTS FALL ON THE GROUP AND RISE ON BENAZIR BHUTTO STANDING ALONE UNDER A SPOTLIGHT.

BHUTTO   I became slowly, slowly sucked into it.

LIGHTS FALL ON BHUTTO AND RISE ON A TALIBAN OFFICIAL READING THE RULES IMPOSED ON KABUL.

PHOTO'S OF BHUTTO'S RETURN AND ASSASSINATION ARE PLAYED OUT ON SCREENS IN THE BACKGROUND.

TALIBAN 1   The following are now banned. Television, kite-flying, homing pigeons, music, dancing, singing, American haircuts, toothpaste, chess, marbles, cigarettes, sorcery, photography.

BHUTTO   It started out with a little fuel. Then it became machinery.

TALIBAN 1   Shop keepers must not wrap goods in paper, lest they inadvertently use pages from the Holy Quran.

All men must grow their beards the required two fists long. Western dress is banned. Men will wear salwar kamerz.

BHUTTO   They needed parts for captured helicopters and tanks. Logistics.

TALIBAN 1   All those sisters who are working in government offices are hereby informed to stay at home until further notice. Since satar is of great importance in Islam, all sisters are seriously asked to cover their faces and the whole of their body when going out. They will be escorted at all times by a male member of their family; boys from four up are acceptable.

BHUTTO   Then I started sanctioning the money.

TALIBAN 1   Taxi drivers are prohibited from stopping for any woman not wearing a full Iranian style burqa.

BHUTTO   Once I gave the go-ahead that they should get money I don't know how much money they were given. It was just carte blanche.

TALIBAN 1   Any sister found washing clothes in the river will be escorted back to her home in a respectful, Muslim manner and her husband severely punished.

Education for girls is against Sharia.

BHUTTO   The ISI kept telling me the closer the links the more they could control them. And I listened.

TALIBAN 1   Only boys under the age of ten can search a woman at checkpoints.

Any tailor found taking measurements of a woman is subject to no less than six months imprisonment.

This is Radio Sharia. Assalamu Alaikum.

SCENE 3

LANGLEY.

AN AIDE IS SITTING BEHIND HER DESK, WRITING.

THE PHONE RINGS.

AIDE   ALEC.(LISTENS) Please hold. (SHE PUSHES ANOTHER BUTTON) Sir, I've got Major General Elfatih Erwa on the phone. (PAUSE) Yes, sir. Sudan. Sir, I think he wants to talk about bin Laden. (PAUSE) Yes, sir. (SHE HITS ANOTHER BUTTON) General, please hold for the Director.

SHE PRESSES ANOTHER BUTTON.

ENTER CIA DIRECTOR.

DIRECTOR   What line's he on?

AIDE   Three.

DIRECTOR   There's a translator on the other end.

AIDE   Yes, sir.

HE POINTS TO A SECOND PHONE AND THE PAIR PICK THEM UP TOGETHER.

DIRECTOR   Major General. Good morning.

AIDE   (TRANSLATING) Good morning, Director. It is good to speak to you.

DIRECTOR   Not at all. I hope everything is alright?

AIDE   (PAUSE) Yes, Mr. Director. The Sudanese government is looking forward to friendly relations with the US We've been doing some gardening.

DIRECTOR   (LOOKING AT THE AIDE) You get that right?

AIDE   Yes, sir.

DIRECTOR   (BACK INTO THE PHONE) Yes, Major. Gardening.

AIDE   (PAUSE) We think it will be safe to reopen the embassy…

DIRECTOR   You know we can't do that Major. The safety of our embassy staff is paramount.

AIDE   (PAUSE) Indeed. We too are concerned with their safety.

DIRECTOR   The government of the United States cannot resume diplomatic relations with the Sudanese government while you harbour and support terrorists, Major.

AIDE   (PAUSE) The Sudanese government has no part in…

DIRECTOR   The Sudanese government is a myth, Major. The Sudanese government helped Osama bin Laden move several tons of explosives into Yemen, Somalia and god knows where else. The Saudis have told you, the President has told you, now I'm telling you. While bin Laden is allowed to stay in your country, there is no relationship with the US.

AIDE   (PAUSE) What would you have me do, Director? Osama bin Laden has broken no laws in Sudan. He is a respected guest and I remind you, sir…

DIRECTOR   Elfatih, the guy's bad news. Sooner or later. The Saudis aren't going to let him stay there and the President's not going to either. Even he's going to come down on this one eventually.

AIDE   (PAUSE) We have offered bin Laden to the Saudis.

DIRECTOR   Say that again?

AIDE   (PAUSE) We have offered bin Laden to Saudi Arabia. They turned us down.

DIRECTOR   I understand.

AIDE   (PAUSE) We would be willing, at this time, to turn him over to the United States if it can be done in secret.

DIRECTOR   We can't do that, Elfatih. You know that. We don't have enough to indict him at this time. The President himself has ruled on it. Elfatih, listen. You're a reformer. We get that. And frankly, we'd like to work with you. I know the position you're in. The position your country is in with regards to bin Laden.

AIDE   (PAUSE) He is a good Muslim.

DIRECTOR   He's a terrible Muslim Elfatih. You have to get rid of him.

AIDE   (PAUSE) Where would we send him?

DIRECTOR   We don't care. Just don't let him go to Somalia.

AIDE   (PAUSE) He will probably go to Afghanistan.

DIRECTOR   (SHRUGS) Let him.

SCENE 4

AFGHANISTAN.

KHALILI'S HOME. KHALILI IS WAITING. HIS WIFE COMES OUT.

LEILA   Is that him?

KHALILI   We will have tea out here. It's too nice a day to be spoiled.

ENTER MASSOUD.

THE TWO EMBRACE.

KHALILI   Commander.

MASSOUD   Here we are again.

KHALILI   And you are always welcome. The withdraw from Kabul?

MASSOUD   A success. It is not difficult to outflank numbers.

KHALILI   Sit, sit. You mustn't see this as a defeat.

MASSOUD   It is a loss, yes. But I understand your point.

KHALILI   These mullahs…

MASSOUD   It is not the mullahs. They are… Yes, they are naive. They are… they are warriors. But this is not a religious movement. Don't let anyone tell you that. You should have seen them marching…. completely…

ENTER LEILA.

SHE IS CARRYING TEA.

LEILA   Commander.

MASSOUD   This is your wife?

KHALILI   You met at our wedding.

MASSOUD   Yes but you were young, this must be a new one!

LEILA   We were all young. It is good to have you here, Commander. Even for these reasons. You are welcome to stay as long as you like.

MASSOUD   Thank you. You are very kind. But then, you must be if you're married to this old goat.

KHALILI   A goat knows where to graze, at least.

LEILA   Drink your tea. (TO MASSOUD) You are most welcome.

EXIT LEILA.

KHALILI   You will leave, maybe the King…? Others have gone already. Haq…

MASSOUD   I cannot leave. This is my country. How would I return? No. Afghanistan is where I live.

KHALILI   Then you will fight?

MASSOUD   It is what we have learnt, old friend. It is what we have learnt. And I still have a fight in me.

A UNOCAL BALL ROLLS ONTO THE STAGE. THE BOY RUNS OUT TO GET IT. MASSOUD PICKS IT UP AND LOOKS AT IT.

KHALILI   They are everywhere.

MASSOUD   UNOCAL?

KHALILI   Oil.

BOY   Can I have my ball please?

KHALILI   Leave the Commander!

MASSOUD   No, no. You can use this?

BOY   I can keep up. Ten times.

MASSOUD   No? Really? I can do twenty.

BOY   I can do twenty too.

MASSOUD   I believe you. Go over there and practice. I will come and we will practice together.

THE BOY TAKES THE BALL.

KHALILI   We can beat them. The Taliban?

MASSOUD   The Taliban? Yes. We can beat them. It's the other countries I'm worried about.

SCENE 5

AFGHANISTAN.

MILLAR IS TOURING AFGHANISTAN WITH AN ARMED GUARD, TRYING TO GET THE PIPELINE UP.

TALIBAN 1   Stop!

TALIBAN 2   Stop where you are!

KIDS MILL ABOUT, INTERESTED IN THE AMERICAN AND UNAFRAID OF THE MEN WITH GUNS.

MILLAR   Easy with the guns, easy with the guns!

GUARD   He has papers.

THE TALIBAN SEARCH HIM QUICKLY.

MILLAR   Easy. Easy. What's the damn hurry?

TALIBAN 2   Five o'clock is prayer time.

MILLAR   You're American?

TALIBAN 2   I was.

MILLAR   Hey, hey, that's great. Listen I've got the papers. I've been holding meetings in Jalaalabad. Tell him.

TALIBAN 2   He's fine. He's just stupid.

TALIBAN 1   Yes.

MILLAR   What are you doing out here?

TALIBAN 2   Answering the call of Allah. How are the Mets?

MILLAR   The Mets. Yeah, they're doing well. Not gonna win the pennant or anything but you know.

TALIBAN 2   Yeah.

MILLAR   Listen, I'm… You know. There a lot of you guys out here?

TALIBAN 2   Americans?

MILLAR   Non-Afghans.

TALIBAN 2   We are Muslims. We are Pakistani, Arabs, Europeans.

MILLAR   Yeah? Listen. I've… We've got these balls. Footballs. For the kids. You know, from my company. Promotions. You think it'll be alright?

TALIBAN 2   He wants to give the children footballs.

TALIBAN 1   As long as they stay away from the mines.

TALIBAN 2   (TO MILLAR) Sure.

MILLAR NODS TO THE GUARD AND HE DISTRIBUTES FOOTBALLS TO THE CHILDREN. THEY RUN AROUND THE STAGE CHASING THE BALLS, PLAYING KEEP UP. THE STAGE IS A SWARM OF SMALL CHILDREN PLAYING WITH ORANGE UNOCAL BALLS.

MILLAR   So, you know, you think you can get me a sit-down with anyone. Been out here a week now and not getting any traction.

MILLAR IS LOST IN THE CROWD OF CHILDREN.

EXIT MILLAR.

ENTER ALBRIGHT.

LIGHTS UP ON MADELINE ALBRIGHT. THE SECRETARY OF STATE ADDRESSES THE AUDIENCE.

ALBRIGHT   The conditions of the camps are deplorable. And the thing is; if this is what it's like in Pakistan, what is it like inside the country, inside Taliban controlled areas? There are fifty five thousand widows in Kabul alone. Fifty five thousand women looking after some four hundred thousand children and they're unable to work, unable to walk the streets without risking beatings from the religious police. These actions; these people, the Taliban, they're deplorable.

WE HEAR THE NOISE OF A GULFSTREAM POWERING DOWN.

LIGHTS DOWN ON ALBRIGHT.

EXIT ALBRIGHT.

ENTER RICHARDSON, INDERFURTH, AND SIMONS.

THE STEPS OF THE PLANE EXTEND AND RICHARDSON EXITS. THE CHILDREN START TO DISPERSE. THE TALIBAN GUARD STEPS FORWARD.

EXIT CHILDREN.

TALIBAN 2   Mr. Richardson.

RICHARDSON That's right.

TALIBAN 2   This way please.

THEY LEAD HIM OVER TO SOME CHAIRS.

TALIBAN 2   Please, sit.

ENTER RABBANI AND OTHERS.

CARRYING RIFLES THEY WALK PAST RICHARDSON AND KNEEL IN PRAYER. RICHARDSON IS FORCED TO WATCH.

THE PRAYER FINISHED, RABBANI STANDS AND HEADS OVER TO RICHARDSON.

RABBANI Ambassador Richardson.

RICHARDSON Mullah Rabbani.

RABBANI Please, sit.

THEY ALL SIT.

INDERFURTH Mullah Omar won't be joining us?

RABBANI He does not meet with non-Muslims, I'm afraid, he is a very devout man. A great man.

SIMONS Also, he never leaves Kandahar.

RABBANI This is also true.

RICHARDSON Mullah Rabbani. There are many in my government who think I should not be here. They think we should not have come. But Bill, the President, he feels and, I guess, we feel as well, that any talk is better than no talk. Only Nixon can go to China.

RABBANI I do not…

SIMONS We are happy to talk. We would like to open talks with the Taliban.

RABBANI You must recognize the Taliban as the rightful rulers of Afghanistan.

INDERFURTH We can't do that.

RICHARDSON Mullah Rabbani. Osama bin Ladin is in Afghanistan. You know this, we know this. He's a bad guy. We have evidence that he has a terrorist network, that he's conducted terrorist acts, that he's using your country as a base and we want you to turn him over to us. We would then legally find a way for this to happen.

RABBANI Pakistan, Saudi Arabia, these are your allies. They have both recognized the Taliban.

INDERFURTH That can never happen, Mullah Rabbani. Not while Osama bin Ladin is the country. This man, he issued a fatwa against the United States. Twice. A fatwa against Americans everywhere!

RABBANI The man is not an Alim. I don't understand. He has no credentials to issue a fatwa.

SIMONS   He's with you. He's not obeying you, whatever you told him, not to be politically active. There's this fatwa in February which says that it's an individual's obligation to kill Americans. Americans!

RICHARDSON If you can't hand him over to us. At least expel him.

PAUSE.

RABBANI   No.

LIGHTS DOWN ON THE GROUP. RICHARDSON ADDRESSES THE AUDIENCE.

RICHARDSON (TA)   It appears we have a breakthrough. I believe the Afghan people want this war to end. I saw it in their eyes.

SCENE 6

SCREENS TO EITHER SIDE OF THE STAGE SHOW NUCLEAR BLASTS.

UN WORKER (TA)   Within weeks of Ambassador to the United Nations Bill Richardson's visit, however, India conducts a series of nuclear tests followed closely by Pakistan's own tests, proving an escalation in the area is imminent.

MASSOUD ENTERS AND LOOKS AT THE SCREENS. THE SCREENS CHANGE TO PICTURES OF THE EMBASSY ATTACKS IN KENYA AND TANZANIA.

HAZARA 1 (TA) Days later members of al Qaeda attacked US embassies in Kenya and Tanzania in coordinated suicide attacks that killed over 200 people and injured another 5000 more.

THE SCREENS CHANGE TO PICTURES OF THE MASSACRE AT MAZAR-I-SHARIF.

HAZARA 2 (TA) The very next day, while the world is focused on

East Africa, Taliban forces aided by al Qaeda troops lay siege to the city of Mazar-i-Sharif in what is to become a common practice of global strategy.

Battles between the Northern Alliance and the Taliban were commonplace, and a failed attempt to capture the city the year before had led to the Taliban's worst defeat. This time, however, their goal was not control, but eradication.

SEVERAL PEOPLE ARE SPOT LIT, FACES ONLY TO GIVE TESTIMONY.

UN WORKER   They broke into UN headquarters and dismantled the communications. That's the first thing they did, across the city, so no one could get word out.

HAZARA 1   They were shooting men. Everywhere. They rode around the city in their jeeps, they kept saying…

HAZARA 2   I gave a man up. I didn't know. They just asked me, "Is he Hazara, is he Hazara?" I told them he was.

HAZARA 1   "Tell us who are Hazaras. Tell us or we will kill you all."

TALIBAN 1   Hazaras have three options. They can become Sunnis, they can go to the Islamic Republic of Iran, or they can be killed.

HAZARA 3   They came into the hospital and went bed to bed, shot all the patients and then shot the relatives visiting them.

OMAR Shias are like Christians and Jews. They are infidels. Once you kill them, their wives and their property are yours.

TALIBAN 2   I don't know if I'll go to heaven now. I was going door to door, shooting whoever answered. I shot the men as they answered the door. Twenty nine houses without a problem but at the thirtieth house I shot the man answering the door. His wife, she was by his side, she was speaking Pashto. I have killed a Pashton. A Sunni. I do not know if I will go to heaven now.

HAZARA 4   They were asking people questions. Sunni or Shia. They asked how many verses of the Quran you said during prayers. If you said two in the evening, you were shot.

UN WORKER (TA)   It is clear that not only were the Taliban unwilling to help America in their bid to capture bin Laden, they were unwilling to share the country with anyone else as well.

THE LIGHTS OF AMERICAN MISSILES AND SMOKE FILL THE STAGE.

SCENE 7

THE STAGE CLEARS, LEAVING ONLY MASSOUD AND A FEW CHAIRS.

MASSOUD IS READING A PIECE OF PAPER.

ENTER KHALILI, INDERFURTH, AND OTHER CIA MEN.

KHALILI   Commander.

MASSOUD   Mr. Secretary.

INDERFURTH Assistant Secretary, I'm afraid. This is a beautiful place. You don't normally travel outside Afghanistan.

MASSOUD   Desperate times call for desperate measures.

INDERFURTH Indeed. Shall we sit? (THEY SIT) Afghanistan has been delivered to fanatic extremists, terrorist mercenaries, drug mafias, and professional murderers.

MASSOUD   Yes.

INDERFURTH You wrote that, in a letter to us. After the bombings in East Africa. I'm not misquoting you?

MASSOUD   Mr. Assistant Secretary…

INDERFURTH Rick, please.

MASSOUD   I am Ingrid Bergman, perhaps? Rick. Afghanistan is at war. We are at war with the Taliban, we are at war with Pakistan intelligence, and with bin Laden. Who you are also at war with. We need America's help and we are on the same side.

SIMONS   We have a common enemy. Let's work together. We want to capture bin Laden.

MASSOUD   Capture bin Laden?

INDERFURTH We've got intelligence.

KHALILI   Do you think, if we could have attacked bin Laden we wouldn't have? Do you think we would be waiting for US permission?

MASSOUD   Rick, Mr. Assistant Secretary, even if we succeeded in what you are asking for, that will not solve the bigger problem that is growing. Look at this.

MASSOUD HANDS HIM THE PAPER.

INDERFURTH What is this?

MASSOUD   This is the list of atrocities committed by the Taliban. Look at it! Kayan Valley: forty thousand people without homes; Shamali, one hundred and forty thousand.

INDERFURTH This is the UN list?

MASSOUD   The United States outlook on this is myopic. It is not the Taliban we are fighting. The Taliban cannot fight this kind of war, not at this level. We are fighting Arabs, Pakistanis. These people, they fight carefully, they aim. They fight until they die. This is not a war with just one man.

INDERFURTH I understand.

MASSOUD   The Taliban's extreme actions have cracked the Pashtuns. An average Pashtun mullah is asking – he knows the history and simply has a question: Why are there no schools? Why is there no education for women? Why are women not allowed to work? It is a totally separate story whether Osama is a popular figure outside Afghanistan or not, but inside Afghanistan, actually he is not!

SIMONS   I think we can all hear that.

MASSOUD   For myself, for my colleagues and for us totally, he is a criminal. He is a person who has committed crimes against our people. Perhaps in the past there was some type of respect for Arabs. People would consider them as Muslims. They had come as guests. But now they are seen as criminals. They are seen as tyrants. They are seen as cruel. Similarly, the reaction is the same against the Pakistani Taliban. The resentment is from the grassroots, from the bottom, from the ulama.

INDERFURTH I think we understand your frustration.

MASSOUD   These talks. Today, they keep talking about the Taliban and the Northern alliance as warring factions. This is not the case. We erred, yes, Our shortcomings were a result of political innocence, inexperience, vulnerability, victimization, bickering, and inflated egos, but by no means does this justify the whirlwind of foreign interest, deception, great-gamesmanship, and internal strife that our so called Cold War allies have done to undermine this just victory. The United States is the only country in the world to have an international charter based on human rights. Why not act on it? Everything should be shared, these are our slogans – what we believe in. We believe in moderate Islam, and of course, they believe in extremism.

INDERFURTH What can we do to help?

MASSOUD   First, political support. Let us reopen our embassy in Washington. This is issue one. We need humanitarian assistance that is not wasted in Pakistan for administration costs or in the UN system. Food, medicine, and of course financial assistance. This is what we need. Our intelligence structure is preoccupied with tactical information that we need. That is our priority. We do not see any problem to working directly against the terrorists, but we have very, very limited resources.

PAUSE.

SIMONS   We can offer you more secure communications, listening devices, and other non-lethal spy gear.

SCENE 8

AFGHANISTAN.

PRINCE TURKI AND NASEEM RANA EXIT FROM AIRCRAFT.

ENTER MULLAH OMAR, MULLAH RABBANI, AND OTHERS.

RABBANI   Prince Turki. Welcome to Afghanistan.

TURKI I wish I could say the same. This is Naseem Rana. He is chief of Pakistani Intelligence.

ENTER WAITER.

THEY WAVE HIM TOWARDS THE SEATS AND THEY SIT. OMAR IS RETICENT. WATER IS PLACED ON THE TABLE.

RABBANI Sit, sit, we will bring you tea, yes?

TURKI Perhaps Mullah Omar does not think our hospitality is important.

RANA I'm sure that…

TURKI I believe the leader of all Muslims can speak for himself? Hmm? We have been waiting for you. You gave us your word that you were going to give Osama bin Laden to us? Did, perhaps, the Mullah lie?

RANA I think that…

RABBANI What the Prince surely means…

OMAR I have never told a lie in my life. I never told you I would hand over Osama. He is our guest. It is not tradition to ask the guest to leave. And where would he go? He would be arrested!

TURKI You think perhaps he shouldn't be? The man has issued a fatwa on the royal family. You think he shouldn't?

OMAR Why are you doing this? Why are you persecuting and harassing this courageous and valiant Muslim? You are keeping troops on sacred soil. Instead of doing that, why don't you put your hands in ours and let us go together and liberate the Arabian Peninsula from the infidel soldiers!

TURKI Is this you speaking, or perhaps your 'guest'? Might I remind you of the friend that Saudi Arabia has been to Afghanistan? It was us, the only Muslims in the world, who stood side by side with the Mujahideen against the Soviets. Us who helped with reconstruction. Us who helped you with arms, with supplies. Will we not do this again? What has Osama ever done except turn the world against you?

OMAR I am so angry, I am fearful of what I will say to you.

HE REACHES OUT AND PICKS UP THE WATER PITCHER,

THEN POURS IT OVER HIS HEAD. EVERYONE IS SHOCKED AND TAKEN ABACK.

OMAR (CONT.) You know, you are an American pimp. Leave this place immediately.

THE PRINCE RISES TO LEAVE.

TURKI What you are doing today is going to bring great harm, not just to you but to Afghanistan.

THE PRINCE STEPS FORWARD TO CENTRE STAGE, A SPOT LIGHTING HIM.

TURKI (CONT., TA)   He was much changed. He made decisions arbitrarily and capriciously and once made, he was not interested in revising them. The Taliban have become fanatics. There is nothing more we can do for them.

SCENE 9

THE WHITE HOUSE.

CLINTON IS ALONE BEHIND HIS DESK.

CLINTON (TA) By the end of the millennium it was clear to everyone involved that the Taliban had been taken over by al Qaeda. The rise of Arab fighters in forward Taliban movements, their success in battles, driving the Northern Alliance further and further into the mountains, and the growing harshness of their actions against their own people marked a shift in both policy and practice. And a plan…

ENTER INDERFURTH.

INDERFURTH Mr. President.

CLINTON   Rick. Come in. I was just going over our numbers.

INDERFURTH Yes, Mr. President.

CLINTON   I really can't see that the American people are interested in all this.

INDERFURTH   No, sir.

CLINTON   Milosevic, the millennium thing, but all they care about…

INDERFURTH   You wanted an Afghan briefing, Mr. President.

CLINTON   I rather think you wanted to give me one.

INDERFURTH   (HANDING OVER PAPERS) Yes, sir.

CLINTON READS.

CLINTON   This is what you think?

INDERFURTH   It's the intelligence, Mr. President.

CLINTON   This is all pretty circumstantial.

INDERFURTH   Mr. President. There is absolutely no doubt that al Qaeda now has considerable sway over the Taliban, if not outright control. They're not listening to Pakistan, they're not listening to the Saudis. This is… Mr. President. This drought that the country is suffering. This is the worst thing that could have hit a land that was already pretty chewed up as it was. The Taliban are losing control. They're having to swing more and more to their right just in order to…

CLINTON   Yeah, yeah. I get it, Rick.

INDERFURTH   Mr. President. Sooner or later we're going to have to get bin Laden. We're going to have to, and he knows it. He's forcing the Taliban to cut off absolutely everyone we have an influence over.

ENTER ABU HAFS.

HAFS ADDRESSES THE AUDIENCE.

ABU HAFS (TA) We told Mullah Omar that we knew astrology. We told him that he could cure the drought with an alignment of stars. We could have told him anything. These were simple people.

CLINTON   The CIA are working with Massoud?

INDERFURTH   They're in the region.

CLINTON   We need to catch him alive, that's what we need. We need to have bin Laden on trial and when we do, we need an open and shut case. We're gonna need more evidence.

INDERFURTH And the Taliban?

SCENE 10

AFGHANISTAN / EGYPT / QATAR / PAKISTAN.

CLINTON (TA) When the Taliban took power in 1997, Mullah Omar issued a statement regarding Afghan national treasures.

OMAR It is necessary for us and all officials of the Islamic Emirate of Afghanistan to protect these valuable artefacts, which express the high and the low points of our country at various stages of its history.

CLINTON (TA) By two thousand however, he appeared to change his mind.

OMAR On the basis of consultation between the religious leaders of the Islamic Emirate of Afghanistan, the religious judgments of the ulama, and the ruling of the Supreme Court, all statues and non-Islamic shrines located in the different parts of the country must be destroyed. These statues have been and remain shrines of infidels, and these infidels continue to worship and respect these shrines. Allah almighty is the only real shrine and all false shrines should be smashed.

BACKDROP SHOWS A PICTURE OF THE BAMIYAN BUDDHAS.

ENTER MULLAH RABBANI, SHEIKH YOUSSEF AL QARADAWI, MUFTI NASR FADID WASEL, AND COLONEL IMAN.

CLINTON (TA) At the heart of the edict were the Buddhas of Bamiyan, two one thousand seven hundred year old statues rising to over 180 feet. Even as dynamite and TNT were packed around their bases, Muslim scholars from across the world, including those within the Taliban itself, protested in vain with Omar.

LIGHTS UP ON ALL FOUR MEN. ALL ON TELEPHONES. OMAR STANDS CENTRE STAGE, ANSWERING THEM.

RABBANI   Tell him Mullah Rabbani respectfully wants to talk to him.

QARADAWI   I am a respected scholar on… Yes, I'll hold.

WASEL As Egypt's highest Muslim authority, I respectfully ask to…

IMAN   Colonel Iman of Pakistan's Security agency for Mullah Omar.

RABBANI   You must stop this, Mullah Omar. This cannot be the will of Allah. Afghanistan… Our people have had these treasures for centuries. This is not about idolatry…

OMAR   I am not the statue seller, I am the sculpture destroyer.

WASEL Yes, images are not to be displayed but…

QARADAWI   …it is not Islamic to ignore the past, it is not Islamic to ignore history.

RABBANI   It is not our place to do this. Please, this is not the way.

OMAR   I am being advised.

WASEL Where in the Quran does it say that we have the right to destroy history? Where in the Quran does it say national heritage is idolatry?

QARADAWI   The world will condemn the Taliban for this. The Islamic community does not support these ideas.

RABBANI   Who is advising you?

OMAR   Arabs, and two mullahs from Karachi.

WASEL Afghanistan is the centre of the religious world. It is the birthplace of Buddhism, it is the home of Zoroastrianism…

OMAR   Allah came to me in my dream at night and ordered me to do this. I'm sorry, I cannot disappoint Allah.

BLACKOUT ON WASEL AND RABBANI.

QARADAWI   These Taliban have absolutely no knowledge about Islam. They are so naïve, they really can be influenced.

BLACKOUT ON QARADAWI.

IMAN   I did not even ask. He had made up his mind.

BLACKOUT ON IMAN.

BLACKOUT ON OMAR.

FADEOUT ON THE BUDDHAS.

MUSIC TO BLACKOUT.

SCENE 11

DARKNESS.

WE HEAR MEN SHOUTING, THE BANGING OF CLOSED DOORS, RUNNING FOOTSTEPS. A GUNSHOT LIGHTS THE SCENE BRIEFLY REVEALING A MAN, FLEEING.

WE HEAR WOMEN AND CHILDREN CRYING.

THERE ARE MORE GUNSHOTS AND LIGHTS. THE MAN IS DEAD.

THE CHILDREN ARE SCREAMING NOW, THEIR WORDS UNRECOGNISABLE. THE FINAL GUNSHOTS SILENCE THEM.

MASSOUD (TA) The murder of the family of Abdul Haq by al Qaeda is followed quickly by the assassination of Abdul Ahad Karzai, father of the future Prime Minister.

Pressure on the Pakistani government and harassment by the ISI force old warriors out of retirement and back into Afghanistan. Meanwhile, Massoud's forces gather to face what they fear might be their final battle.

And for the first time, Massoud himself travels to Europe in hope of securing a meeting with the European Council.

SCENE 12

AFGHANISTAN.

LIGHTS UP ON THE REST OF THE STAGE REVEALS A MEETING WITH MASSOUD'S MEN.

KHALILI IS READING FROM A BOOK OF HAFIZ.

KHALILI   "This dark night is pregnant with tomorrow. You too do not know what will be the child. The world is a clear story, full of deception. You do not know what will be the trick of tomorrow morning."

MASSOUD   They are here? The reporters?

KHALILI   Waiting outside.

AMBULLAH   Commander, I'm sorry, but this is not a good idea.

MASSOUD   They are Arabs?

KHALILI   They have passports. From Belgium. They have been waiting a long time.

AMBULLAH   I can send them away?

MASSOUD   We will need all the help we can get in the coming months. Show them in.

EXIT AMBULLAH.

KHALILI   Do we lose Afghanistan?

MASSOUD   Be brave. It is a big offensive. The goal is to get Badakshan and get us out.

AIDE   And the Pakistanis?

MASSOUD   From the madrassas, naturally. But this is the war of al Qaeda. The Pakistanis never succeed at anything. Do you ever see Arabs succeeding in anything? The defeated ones become heroes. We need all the help we can.

ENTER AMBULLAH, KARIM TOUZANI, AND KACEM BAKKALI.

THE PAIR START TO SET UP THEIR CAMERA EQUIPMENT.

AMBULLAH   Set up anywhere.

MASSOUD   Is he a wrestler or a photographer?

TOUZANI   Are you ready?

MASSOUD   When you are.

TOUZANI   You have had a chance to review the questions?

MASSOUD   Ask me anything you like.

TOUZANI   What would you do with Osama bin Ladin if you captured him?

THE CAMERA EXPLODES IN A FLASH OF LIGHT, BLINDING THE AUDIENCE.

MASSOUD IS BEING CRADLED BY KHALILI, BLOOD COVERING MOST OF HIS UPPER TORSO. HE IS CLEARLY DYING.

THERE IS THE SOUND OF GUNFIRE FROM OUTSIDE.

THE SOPRANO HAS TAKEN HER PLACE AT THE BACK OF THE STAGE.

SCENE 13

IN LINES OF THREE: DOWNSTAGE, IN FRONT OF MASSOUD, AND UPSTAGE OF THE SOPRANO, LARGE SCREEN TVs DISPLAYING REAL TIME NEWS OF THE EVENTS OF 9/11 ARE PUSHED BACK AND FORTH SHOWING THE DEVASTATING EFFECTS WHILE MASSOUD DIES.

A STRING QUARTET IS MOVED ON STAGE.

THE SOPRANO SINGS A REQUIEM TO 'ADAGIO FOR STRINGS' BY BARBER.

Adagio for Strings Requiem.

LYRICS

Our cursed heart, forgotten mind, the land we lost, the arms we raised.

These
Are our blessings
These

Are our homes.

One world we made. One heart that calls
                              You
This cursed heart, this blessed soul, forget me or my name or
my   my soul
Falls
We are like rain. We are like smoke. We are like blessings over
over
        again
                    we're
Falling, we're
                    from the sky.
Fall
Forgo this land, forgive this life, forswear my love, begin this
day, and end this prayer, I breathe this land, I lost my home,
these arms are full, this fire burns, forgive this sky.
Love here.
        Live well.
                    Grow, learn.
                              Die.
So here I find my home is gone
No fear.
I found my breath, I found my time, I found my blessings,
found my land, I have my soul
And so it ends.
And so goes on.

SMOKE POURS ONTO THE STAGE, ENGULFING THE
QUARTET, ETC.

SCENE 14

A SOLE TV REMAINS ON STAGE SHOWING PRESIDENT
BUSH'S SPEECH OF OCT 7TH.

BUSH   Good afternoon. On my orders, the United States military
has begun strikes against al Qaeda terrorist training camps and military

installations of the Taliban regime in Afghanistan. These carefully targeted actions are designed to disrupt the use of Afghanistan as a terrorist base of operations, and to attack the military capability of the Taliban regime.

BREAK.

More than two weeks ago, I gave Taliban leaders a series of clear and specific demands.

BREAK.

None of these demands were met. And now the Taliban will pay a price. By destroying camps and disrupting communications, we will make it more difficult for the terror network to train new recruits and coordinate their evil plans.

BREAK

At the same time, the oppressed people of Afghanistan will know the generosity of America and our allies. As we strike military targets, we'll also drop food, medicine and supplies to the starving and suffering men and women and children of Afghanistan.

The United States of America is a friend to the Afghan people, and we are the friends of almost a billion worldwide who practice the Islamic faith. The United States of America is an enemy of those who aid terrorists and of the barbaric criminals who profane a great religion by committing murder in its name.

BREAK.

Today we focus on Afghanistan, but the battle is broader. Every nation has a choice to make. In this conflict, there is no neutral ground. If any government sponsors the outlaws and killers of innocents, they have become outlaws and murderers, themselves. And they will take that lonely path at their own peril.

BREAK.

We did not ask for this mission, but we will fulfil it. The name of today's military operation is Enduring Freedom. We defend not only our precious freedoms, but also the freedom of people everywhere to live and raise their children free from fear.

BREAK.

To all the men and women in our military - every sailor, every soldier, every airman, every coast-guardsman, every Marine - I say this: Your mission is defined; your objectives are clear; your goal is just. You have my full confidence, and you will have every tool you need to carry out your duty.

BREAK.

The battle is now joined on many fronts. We will not waver; we will not tire; we will not falter; and we will not fail. Peace and freedom will prevail.

Thank you. May God continue to bless America.

BLACKOUT.

SCENE 15

AFGHANISTAN.

THE CENTRE OF THE STAGE IS A DARKENED HUSK, AS THOUGH A SITE OF A BOMB BLAST.

TWO MEN ENTER, BOTH AFGHANS. THOUGH BOTH ARE DRESSED IN AFGHAN DRESS, ONE, THE MAN, IS DRESSED IN CLEAN, NEW-LOOKING CLOTHES, WHILE THE OTHER'S CLOTHES, AND HIS RIFLE, LOOK OLDER.

THE MAN TURNS TO HIS GUARD AND HANDS HIM MONEY.

MAN   Thank you.

GUARD   You want I to wait.

MAN   No, I'll be… I'm fine.

GUARD   Okay.

EXIT GUARD.

THE MAN WALKS TOWARDS THE HOUSE. ANOTHER MAN ENTERS, OLDER, POINTING A GUN AT HIM.

OLD MAN   Stop!

THE MAN STOPS, RAISES HIS HANDS.

MAN   I meant no harm!

OLD MAN   You go now!

MAN   I mean no harm.

OLD MAN   What do you want? You are military? Reporter?

MAN   No. I… I grew up here. This is my home.

OLD MAN You are Afghan?

MAN   I grew up here.

THE OLD MAN SHOULDERS HIS WEAPON, EXTENDS A HAND.

OLD MAN You are coming home, eh?

MAN   Yes.

OLD MAN   From America?

MAN   Yes.

OLD MAN   A lot has happened.

MAN   My father. We planted a tree here. When I was…. Before we left.

OLD MAN   Your father in America?

MAN   He died.

OLD MAN   I'm sorry. My son. He died.

MAN   I thought it might be grown. The tree.

OLD MAN   Not much grows here. The drought. Bombs. You want tea? I'll get you tea.

MAN   No, thank you, it's no bother.

OLD MAN   I'll get you tea. You wait here. (HE TURNS TO GO AND SMILES) Coming home.

EXIT OLD MAN.

SADLY AND SLOWLY THE MAN SITS AT THE EDGE OF THE BURNT GROUND AND RELAXES.

MUSIC: The Lark Ascending (conclusion) by Vaughan Williams.

THE LIGHTS DIM. BEHIND HIM A LARGE TREE GROWS OUT OF THE SCORCHED EARTH, REACHING UP TO FILL THE STAGE.

SCENE 16

THE CAST TAKE THEIR PLACES ON STAGE.

TEEN   There is only one prerogative for the future and that is to make sure it doesn't contain the mistakes of the past.

BRZEZINSKI   There has never been a time when this was more true. There has never been a time when this was more important.

BREZHNEV   After the British, there were the Soviets. After the Soviets…

MASSOUD   …there were the Taliban and with both of them the kind of international crisis that engulfs the world.

MOTHER   If we allow this pattern, if we allow the world to become uninterested in Afghanistan…

TURKI   …we allow it to be uninterested in the future. There is, right now…

ANDROPOV   …the past, staring us in the face. If we let this come to pass, then we are the Soviet forces that killed over a million citizens.

OMAR   We are the Taliban who abused women's rights and massacred a generation.

TARAKI   And we are the past. Repeated over and over again. Here…

BOY   …at the crossroads of the world and at every corner of the coming century.

CURTAINS.

END OF ACT THREE.

Also by

DIRECT

LIGHT

Thomas Alexander

THOMAS ALEXANDER

THE VISITOR

BY

THOMAS ALEXANDER

THE VISITOR

WHEN THE LOVER OF A FAMOUS
WRITER GOES MISSING IN A WAR
RAVAGED COUNTRY, HE BRIBES HIS
WAY INTO A JAIL TO QUESTION HER
HUSBAND, A MISSIONARY, WHO
IS BEING TORTURED AS A TRAIN-
ING EXERCISE BY HIS CAPTORS.

ALONE IN THE CELL, THE TWO
START A DIALOGUE ABOUT THE
NATURE OF BELIEF.

BELIEF IN GOD, LOVE AND POLITICS.

MURDER ME GENTLY

By

Thomas Alexander

*"ONE MAN... ONE WOMAN...
AND THE QUEST FOR JUSTICE
IN AN UNJUST WORLD"*

Modern day Russia through the medium of Film Noir

Blending real life events with comedy and intrigue, *MURDER ME GENTLY*'s unique perspective on the world of Russian Politics as seen through the lens of Flim Noir, spans the assasination of internationally renowned journalists, Putin's reach for the return of Soviet Satelite states, and the inflitration of government by oligarchs and criminals.

Providing a damming indictment of the West's inability to halt Moscow's policy of expansionism *MURDER ME GENTLY* lends a theatrical expose to the very real world of corruption and greed in International politics today.

*A CONMAN, A DISGRACED INTERPOL AGENT, A MA-
FIA BOSS, A CIA SPOOK, AND THE SECRET TO THE
FUTURE ALL UNITE IN AN UNLIKELY ALLIANCE IN
A LOVE AFFAIR THAT WILL DEFINE THE FATE OF
THE WORLD IN* THOMAS ALEXANDER'S

... MURDER ME ... GENTLY!

GRE⬛T

GREAT

BY

THOMAS ALEXANDER

A REMOTE ROOM IN THE THROES OF WINTER.

THE ONCE GREAT MAN LIVES ALONE NOW WITH HIS SON,

AN OLD FRIEND HAS COME TO VISIT. HE HAS CLIMBED UP FROM THE VILLAGE IN ORDER TO OFFER THE OLD MAN ONE LAST CHANCE TO ESCAPE THE ENCROACHING WINTER THAT IS ABOUT TO TAKE HIM, STIRRING UP MEMORIES OF BETTER TIMES AND THE WARMTH OF SUMMER.

BEGAT

By

THOMAS ALEXANDER

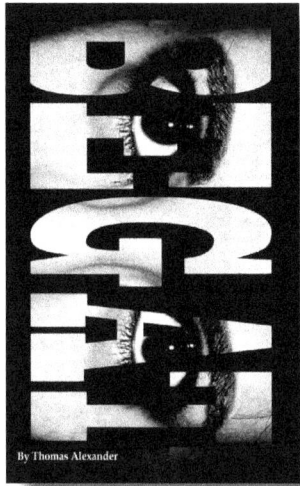

By Thomas Alexander

IN A COUNTRY, AFTER THE WAR, A JUDGE THROWS A DINNER PARTY, SEEKING SUPPORT AGAINST A POWERFUL MINISTER WHO HAS RAPED AND KILLED A SERVANT GIRL.

BUT THE JUDGE HIMSELF IS THE TARGET TONIGHT, AND THE SHADOW OF THE WAR HE SO DESPERATELY WANTS TO LEAVE BEHIND THREATENS TO ENGULF HIS FAMILY AS A YOUNG WOMAN SEEKS REVENGE FOR THE SINS OF HIS PAST.

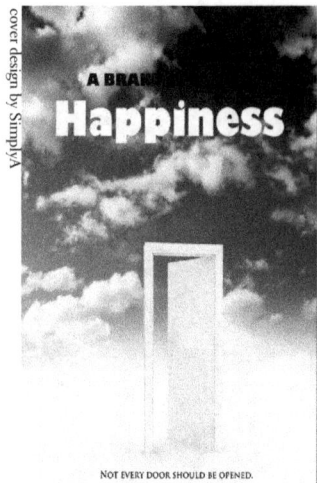

A BRAND

Happiness

NOT EVERY DOOR SHOULD BE OPENED.

HAPPINESS

BY

THOMAS ALEXANDER

ON A REMOTE HEADLAND IN NORTH WALES A MAN AND HIS PARAPLEGIC SON DREAM OF LIFE BEYOND THE CONFINES OF THEIR FOUR WALLS.

BUT WHEN A WOMAN OFFERS THEM THE ESCAPE THEY SO CRAVE THEY FIND THEY ARE BOUND BY MORE THEN THEIR DREAMS.

THE JEALOUSY OF A BORED POLICE-MAN AND THE KINDNESS OF A MAIL ORDER BRIDE SET THEM ON A PATH OF HOPE AND DESTRUCTION.

THE LAST CHRISTMAS

THE LAST CHRISTMAS

By

THOMAS ALEXANDER

IT'S NEWS!

WHEN AN EMBATTLED NEWSROOM RECEIVES A POTENTIALLY EARTH SHATTERING STORY MINUTES BEFORE AIR ON CHRISTMAS DAY THE CAREFUL EQUILIBRIUM OF THE TEAM IS SHATTERED AND OLD DIVIDING LINES COME TO THE FORE, TURNING CO-WORKER AGAINST CO-WORKER.

SET IN REAL TIME AND INCORPORATING ACTUAL AND INTERCHANGEABLE NEWS EVENTS THE LAST CHRISTMAS PITS SOCIAL POLITICS AGAINST JOURNALISTIC INTEGRITY IN A BATTLE OF THE ETHICS.

GOD

By

THOMAS ALEXANDER

WHEN THE NAMED PARTNER OF A SMALL LAW FIRM DIES, LEAVING LARGE DEBT, THE REMAINING MISFITS OF THE FIRM ARE FORCED TO TAKE ON JUST ABOUT ANY CLIENT AVAILABLE, INCLUDING A LITIGIOUS SOCCER-MUM WHO WOULD LIKE TO SUE GOD FOR THE DEATH OF HER HUSBAND – HIT BY A LIGHTNING BOLT ON THE 15TH HOLE OF A MUNICIPAL GOLF COURSE.

THE TRIAL BECOMES COMPLICATED HOWEVER, WHEN AN INDIGENT WITH NO BACKGROUND AND A CANNY KNACK OF KNOWING EVERYONE'S BACKGROUND ENTERS THE COURTROOM CLAIMING TO BE 'GOD'.

BATTING BACK AND FORE BETWEEN THE COURTROOM AND THE PERSONAL LIVES OF THE LAWYERS, 'GOD' IS A FAST PACED COURTROOM DRAMA/COMEDY THAT USES ORIGINAL STAGING AND NON-LINEAR STORYTELLING TO PROVIDE A LIGHTHEARTED, BUT COMPLEX SOCIAL DRAMA.

THE FAMILY

By

THOMAS ALEXANDER

TODAY, FOR THE FIRST TIME IN LONGER THAN ANYONE CAN REMEMBER, THE FAMILY ARE GATHERING. THEY ARE GATHERING TO CELEBRATE THE ENGAGEMENT OF THE MATRIARCHAL NIECE, THEY ARE GATHERING TO CELEBRATE THE LAST BIRTHDAY OF THE PATRIARCH, THEY ARE GATHERING TO WELCOME HOME THE PRODIGAL SON AND HIS BEAUTIFUL GIRLFRIEND AND THEY ARE GOING TO CELEBRATE ALL THIS WITH A SLIDESHOW.

CANDID PHOTOGRAPHS. PHOTOGRAPHS OF THINGS NO ONE THOUGHT ANYONE ELSE KNEW ABOUT. PHOTOGRAPH TAKEN WHEN NO ONE ELSE WAS THERE.

IT'S ALL COMING OUT TODAY. IN BLACK AND WHITE FOR EVERYONE TO SEE. THE REMNANTS OF CHILD ABUSE, INFIDELITY, LOSS, DESTRUCTION AND MISSED BIRTHDAY PARTIES. IT'S ALL COMING OUT. IT'S GOING TO BE A LONG NIGHT. POSSIBLY FOREVER.

THE RECRUITMENT OFFICER

By

THOMAS ALEXANDER

TOM, A CHARMING YANKEE RECRUITER, COMES TO AN UNSPECIFIED ENGLISH TOWN AND FALLS IN LOVE WITH THE CONFERENCE CENTRE MANAGER, JULIA.

BUT WHAT EXACTLY IS HE RECRUITING FOR? WHY DOES EVERYONE WHO JOINS NEVER COME BACK AND WHAT IS ON THE OTHER SIDE OF THE DOOR

WHERE DO THE RECRUITS GO AFTER SIGNING UP?

AN EXISTENTIAL LOVE STORY THAT ASKS QUESTIONS OF WHO WE ARE, WHAT WE WANT FROM LIFE, AND WHETHER WE'RE GETTING IT, THE RECRUITMENT OFFICER IS A REMODELLING OF THE 1706 PLAY BY GEORGE FARQUHAR. *THE RECRUITING OFFICER.*

Writer's Block

By

Thomas Alexander

Paul Block was once a prolific writer. A recipient of both the Pen and Faulkner-awards and the author of over ten different novels, he was once considered the UK's most up and coming writer until, at the age of forty, he suffered a nervous breakdown.

Ten years later the world has forgotten Paul Block. Holed up in his study he has been working on the same first page of his new novel for nearly five years, kept company by only his maid, a foul mouthed Irish hit-man, a veteran of the battle of Gettysburg and a nineteen forties femme fatale.

Today, all that's going to change. Paul has a busy day ahead of him. First he's going to kill a persistent and charmless young reporter who wants to do a piece on 'writer's block' and then he's going to have a rare visit from his son who's bringing him bad news and a new couch.

With a missing body and a son who hates him, Paul must finally rid himself of his protagonists if he's ever going to stay out of jail, and finish that first page.

THOMAS

Japan, 1945 – A Family At War

When a wandering priest escaping a troubled past is taken in by a prominent family, a quiet city in northern Japan is forced to confront the dark shadows of war seeping into their lives in ways they could never have anticipated.

With its townsmen scattered throughout the farthest ends of a desperate empire in a final defence against the encroaching West, the idyllic northern city of Morioka, far removed from the harsh realities of the front, is largely left to itself.

But when a prominent doctor is conscripted and sent to Manila, his sister is left as head of the household and must deal with a young priest living at the bottom of their garden with a large collection of maps and strange knowledge of English.

As the cold hand of war approaches, each person must choose their own destiny and place in the new world.

THOMAS ALEXANDER

A Scattering of Orphans

THE OTHER SIDE